Why Mark?

The Politics of Resurrection in the First Gospel

Dr. David E. Wiley III

CSS Publishing Company, Inc.
Lima, Ohio

WHY MARK?
THE POLITICS OF RESURRECTION IN THE FIRST GOSPEL

FIRST EDITION
Copyright © 2015
by CSS Publishing Co., Inc.

Unless otherwise marked scripture quotations are from the New Revised Standard Version of the Bible. Copyright 1989 by the Division of Christian Education of the National Council of the Churches of Christ in the USA, Nashville, Thomas Nelson Publishers © 1989. Used by permission. All rights reserved.

Scripture quotations marked (RSV) are from the Revised Standard Version of the Bible, copyrighted 1946, 1952 ©, 1971, 1973, by the Division of Christian Education of the National Council of the Churches of Christ in the USA. Used by permission.

Library of Congress Cataloging-in-Publication Data

Wiley, David E., Dr.
  Why Mark? : the politics of resurrection in the first gospel / Dr. David E. Wiley III.
-- FIRST EDITION.
      pages cm
   ISBN 0-7880-2805-7 (alk. paper)
   1. Bible. Mark--Criticism, interpretation, etc. I. Title.

   BS2585.52.W54   2014
   226.3'06--dc23

                                                      2014024220

For more information about CSS Publishing Company resources, visit our website at www.csspub.com, email us at csr@csspub.com, or call (800) 241-4056.

e-book:
ISBN-13: 978-0-7880-2806-9
ISBN-10: 0-7880-2806-5

ISBN-13: 978-0-7880-2805-2
ISBN-10: 0-7880-2805-7   PRINTED IN USA

For

Phyllis,
Greg, Erica, and Jeff

for their love and support
through the many years of ministry

Table of Contents

Foreword

This book is written for the "critically thinking" person of faith. It grew out of classes populated with laity who were not afraid to ask questions and who were willing to explore the Bible with open minds as well as open hearts.

It began as a study as to why Mark failed to include resurrection appearances at the end of his gospel (a fact many laity in my classes did not know).

It evolved into a study of the person of Mark and why he wrote. Along the way I discovered that Mark wrote as much for political reasons as for theological ones, and that the omission of resurrection appearances after the story of the empty tomb (a seemingly theological issue) had political implications I hadn't expected.

Let me be clear: The gospel of Mark is, in its entirety, the story of the resurrection of Jesus Christ. Although Mark may have no resurrection appearances *after* the story of the empty tomb, he has not omitted the resurrection — nor, I believe, has he omitted resurrection appearances. When one reads the gospel of Mark as a chronology, however, this point can be missed, for the gospel is not a chronological story in the traditional sense. It is, rather, a story that begins at the end, and ends at the beginning. It is an account from a master storyteller, who believes, in its entirety, in the resurrection of Jesus, and who uses his great writing skills to tell the story of Jesus' resurrection in a unique, compelling, and I believe, extremely powerful way. We might even call the gospel of Mark "The Resurrection Gospel."

Even so, this book is not a devotional work, nor is it a study of Jesus (although we will talk much about Jesus and his teachings).

Rather, it is a study of Mark, the author of the gospel of the same name, who was the first to write the story of the "Good News of Jesus Christ [the son of God]." It is a study forty years in the making, as I have been preaching and teaching from Mark throughout the course of my ministry.

Finally, I want to thank all those who shared in my classes over the years and who worked through the questions with me, and a special word of thanks to Paul Semendinger, a lay person who spent countless hours reading various drafts and giving invaluable feedback, and Matt Goodier, who also acted as a reader, editor, and critic.

Introduction

Why Paul?

When Paul wrote the letters that eventually became part of what the Christian church calls scripture, he did not write simply to say "hello" or to tell people what was happening in his life (the way some do today, for example, when they write summaries of their year to include with cards at Christmas). Although Paul included personal information and greetings in his letters, his primary purpose in writing was to answer questions being raised by the communities he had visited, or planned to visit someday, and to address other problems the churches were experiencing regarding practice or doctrine.

Why a "new" testament?

Similarly, when the church decided to compile a corpus of documents that would eventually become Christian canon, it did not do so just because someone thought it would be a nice thing to do. In fact, the early church already had scriptures — the same ones Jesus used — which Christians today commonly call the Old Testament or the Hebrew scriptures.

As the church spread and grew, however, different people began to teach different doctrines and looked to different resources for justification. One such teacher was named Marcion, who lived in the mid-second century — about 125 years after Christ. Marcion — whom Hippolitus says was the son of the bishop of Sinope — taught that the God of Jesus was a different God than the God of the Old Testament, and that Jesus was not fully human but only appeared to be human, among other doctrines. To support his point of view, Marcion promulgated an edited version of Luke's gospel, along with similarly edited letters of Paul. The church ultimately rejected Marcion's teachings, excommunicated him as a heretic, and to counter his limited and edited versions of Luke and Paul, began to consider what works it would deem as authoritative. It ultimately decided to draw its circle as wide as it could with integrity, and included not only all of Luke, but also Matthew, Mark, and John. Similarly, all of the letters thought to be written by Paul were included — not the edited versions of Marcion — along with others purportedly written by Peter, James, and John, along with the Apocalypse of John — and to affirm that the God of the Old Testament was the same God as the God of Jesus, the Hebrew scriptures were included in the Christian canon, as well. All of these works would be necessary, the church taught, in order to present the "whole gospel to the whole world."

Why Mark?

What about Mark? Why did he compose the book we call "gospel"? Did he do it simply because he wanted to tell the story of Jesus — a noble enough task, to be sure — or did he, too, write to address specific problems and issues — theological, political, and otherwise — dogging the early church? Why did he write what he wrote, when he wrote, how he wrote, where he wrote?

Why Mark?

Chapter 1

Starting at the End

I was in my first year of seminary. I was sitting in my first class on the gospels, and the professor was reading from the gospel of Mark. He reached the last chapter where the women arrive at the tomb — finding it empty and a young man sitting outside — and he read these words (from the Revised Standard Version — the New Revised Standard Version had not yet been published):

> And he said to them, "Do not be amazed; you seek Jesus of Nazareth, who was crucified. He has risen, he is not here; see the place where they laid him. But go, tell his disciples and Peter that he is going before you to Galilee; there you will see him, as he told you."
> And they went out and fled from the tomb; for trembling and astonishment had come upon them; and they said nothing to any one, for they were afraid.
> — Mark 16:6-8 (RSV)

"And that is where the gospel of Mark ends," the professor announced to the class.

What do you mean "that's where it ends"? I thought. *What about the rest of the gospel — the verses that say that they went back to tell the others? What about his appearances to the disciples and his ascension to heaven?*

"The oldest manuscripts of the gospel do not include those verses," the professor continued, as if reading my mind. "There are other manuscripts — not as old and not considered as reliable — that have two more sentences included at the end of verse 8. Those sentences are called the 'short ending' of Mark. Still other manuscripts have *twelve* more verses, which are called the 'long ending.'

Most scholars, however, consider both of those endings to be later additions, redacted from the other gospels. It appears that Mark intended to end his story after the words 'and they said nothing to anyone, for they were afraid,' and that he reported no resurrection appearances of Jesus in his gospel."

It was one of the oddest things I'd ever heard.

Atheists, agnostics, and people of other faiths may think that the story of the resurrection of Jesus is odd, but to those of us who had heard and believed the stories of the empty tomb — and of Mary in the garden, the road to Emmaus, the Great Commission, and all the other post-resurrection stories since before we can remember — the idea that Mark would not have any resurrection appearances in his gospel seemed odder still.

There was no hint of this in the first Bible I had been given in the late 1950s as a boy in church — the King James Version. It contained the second half of verse 8 through verse 20, without heading or footnote. To this young Christian, those verses were the standard and accepted conclusion to the gospel.

As a teenager in the 1960s, the preferred Bibles in the churches I attended became the Revised Standard and the Today's English (Good News) Versions. Those versions did have headings that indicated a shorter ending and a longer ending — with footnotes denoting that some ancient manuscripts did not include these endings — but these endings themselves were still included in the body of the text — and nowhere did the footnotes indicate that the endings were not written by Mark.

Sitting there in my seminary class, I wanted to argue with the professor, but under his tutelage a close and critical look at the text made that hard to do. Among other things, he demonstrated that the short ending used language Mark would not. For example, the final word of that passage is "salvation" — the Greek word *soterias*. While that word appears five times in the gospel of Luke, it doesn't appear even once anywhere else in Mark. He also explained that the long ending was an apparent conglomeration of summary sentences taken directly from the endings of Matthew, Luke, and John. Some hands other than Mark's seemed to be at work in these endings, in order to provide what they thought Mark had omitted.

In my mind I still protested. After all, even if *these* endings were not written by Mark, I reasoned, it didn't necessarily mean that Mark intended to conclude his gospel at verse 8. Ancient manuscripts were written on parchment scrolls, and it was well known that the beginning and endings of those rolls would often dry and break off. Indeed, much of what we have of ancient manuscripts are "fragments" and not complete scrolls at all. Perhaps some final portions of the original scroll broke off and were lost. Perhaps these "lost" pages would reveal that Mark originally had an ending in which the women told the disciples the good news and together they went to Galilee, as the young man at the tomb had directed, where they met the risen Lord!

Perhaps.

But what if the oldest manuscripts we have of Mark really *are* complete? What if they accurately reflect what Mark actually wrote? What if Mark *intended* to end his gospel in the middle of verse 8? What would explain why Mark would not include accounts of the risen Lord? Did Mark believe that Jesus had risen, but never appeared to anyone? Did the women really run away and never tell anyone? And how would Mark have known?

I didn't know it at the time, but a life-long quest had begun.

Chapter 2

The Quest for the Historical Mark

Many books have been written on "the quest for the historical Jesus" — the quintessential work being the book of that name by Albert Schweitzer. Unfortunately, in searching for Jesus, we have had to rely on what *others* wrote about him. Unlike the prophets of the Old Testament, we have no books by Jesus' hand. Neither do we have anything dictated by Jesus to others — the way that Paul dictated some of his letters to a scribe or secretary. Whatever Jesus was — a carpenter, a teacher, a preacher, a storyteller, a miracle worker, Son of God, Son of Man — he was not an author or writer. The only words and actions we have of Jesus come to us through the filter of others — people like Matthew, Mark, Luke, John, and Paul. Many of these people had not met Jesus during his lifetime on earth. This includes Paul, for sure, but also Matthew, Luke, and John. Of all the gospel writers, Mark may have been the only one to have known Jesus personally, and his interaction may have been limited to Holy Week alone.

Whether the New Testament authors knew Jesus firsthand or not, however, *our* understanding of Jesus is through *them*. Therefore, in order to understand Jesus, we need to understand the writers themselves — who they were and what biases and perspectives they may have had. Once we better understand the ones who wrote about Jesus, I believe, we will better understand the Jesus of whom they wrote.

Mark is a good place to start because — at least among the synoptic gospel writers (the other two are Matthew and Luke) — Mark was the first. This can be seen most easily, I think, when reading the gospels in parallel. In a Parallel Bible the gospels are placed in columns, side by side. When read this way, it becomes evident that virtually all of Mark is included in the gospels of both Matthew and Luke — much of the time following Mark's order, and sometimes even quoting him word for word. Although they also added to and re-worked Mark's gospel, it appears that they had Mark in front of them when they wrote. This is why we call these three gospels "synoptic" — they look at Jesus through the "same eye."

We don't know what material Mark had in front of *him* when *he* wrote. Was there already an order to the narrative, or did Mark have to create it himself? Was some of it written or did he write down stories others told him? How much was hearsay — stories that had been passed from person to person over a number of years — and how much was from eyewitnesses? Was any of it based on Mark's own personal contact with Jesus?

The best answer to these questions is probably "all of the above," but whatever material Mark may have had in front of him, we can imagine that he re-worked that material in much the same way Matthew and Luke did in order to tell the story he wanted to tell. He had to fashion it into a narrative, deciding how to start it and how to end it, and he certainly chose different ways to start and end than did Matthew and Luke. He had to put the stories he collected into an order, and then write transitions between these stories. He also, at times, had to supply words of interpretation as to what Jesus had meant, such as in Mark 7:19 when Jesus says: "Whatever goes into a person from outside cannot defile" and Mark inserts: "Thus he declared all foods clean."

And he had to decide what to leave out. As opposed to Matthew and Luke, for example, Mark left out stories of

Jesus' birth and upbringing. He catalogued no beatitudes, reported no story of a prodigal son, included no Lord's Prayer — *and he records no resurrection appearances of Jesus after the story of the empty tomb.*

Mark may have left out some of these stories simply because he didn't have access to them. Others, I believe, he left out for specific reasons — reasons we shall explore in the coming pages.

Of course, Mark did not claim to tell the whole story of Jesus. Neither did the other gospel writers. Whoever wrote John even confessed as much:

> But there are also many other things that Jesus did; if every one of them were written down, I suppose that the world itself could not contain the books that would be written.
> — John 21:25

In not telling the whole story, Mark and the other gospel writers stood in good company. The Old Testament authors of First and Second Kings, for example, had done the same thing. When those writers composed their story — sometime after the destruction of the first temple in 587 BC — they hadn't tried to tell the whole history of Israel and Judah. Others had already done that ("Now the rest of the acts of Rehoboam, and all that he did, are they not written in the Book of the Annals of the Kings of Judah?" [1 Kings 14:29; cf also 1 Kings 11:41 and 1 Kings 14:19]). Rather, they selected slices of those histories in order to explain why their temple had been destroyed and why God had allowed them to be carried off to Babylon.

I believe Mark and the others who wrote about Jesus — writing sometime after the destruction of the second temple in AD 70 — took slices of Jesus' life in order to address the issues they faced in those years, including theological issues such as the nature of Jesus' messiahship and political issues such as who should lead the community that came to be known as the church. In so doing, they addressed the early church and, by extension, us today.

As such, Mark was not just an editor or a reporter. He was an artisan who judiciously crafted his narrative, making his points in the ways he depicted the various groups and characters in the story, in the ways he arranged the stories he included, and even through what he left out.

Neither was he Luke, Matthew, or John. He was *Mark*, writing in a particular time for a particular purpose. We might even say that the gospel of Mark is more about Mark and his contemporaries than it is about Jesus and his ministry.

As we look at Mark in this study, we will also look at Luke, Matthew, and others, but primarily to see in what ways they were changed or differed from Mark — and why they may have done so — in order for us to better understand what Mark was trying to say. We shall try to focus on "Mark alone" — to read Mark as Mark — as we explore the questions that compelled him to write, and to discern how he answered them.

Chapter 3

Issues in Reading Mark as Mark

Focusing on Mark and his gospel alone, however, is easier said than done. One concern is what we might call the problem of "harmonization"; another might be called "compartmentalization"; a third, "projection."

Harmonization

One of the reasons we sometimes have problems in understanding what an individual gospel writer is trying to say is because we often blend all of the gospel stories into one single narrative. This is best seen, perhaps, in the way many churches celebrate the Christmas story with children. Angels, shepherds, and Magi all arrive at the manger together, seemingly moments after Jesus was born, even though the shepherds and the Magi never met. In fact, it may have taken the Magi up to twelve months to arrive in Bethlehem — and when they finally did arrive they visited Jesus not in a stable but in a house (Matthew 2:11). We tend to do the same thing with Good Friday (the "seven words from the cross") and the events of Easter Day. We focus on the blended story — harmonizing the separate stories of Matthew, Mark, Luke, and John into one — instead of understanding each gospel on its own in the way its author intended.

Compartmentalization

Alternatively, when we study the Bible today we often do so in short snippets, focusing on the meaning of a particular passage or story in the Bible. This is actually an occupational hazard for clergy as we prepare for a Sunday's sermon by focusing on relatively short selected texts. By concentrating on such sections we may gain great insight into specific teachings of Jesus and their meaning for us today, but in so doing we can miss the thrust of the big picture — that is, the big picture of an individual author and what that author was trying to communicate.

This became particularly clear to me several years ago when I was doing a sermon series focusing on the gospel of Mark. In the months preceding this series I had brushed off my Greek New Testament, taken out the lexicons and grammars I had not used since my days in seminary, and spent an hour a day working my way through the gospel of Mark, writing my own translation as I went along. I then recorded in my own voice what I had translated, copied it onto CD, and distributed it to the entire congregation, asking them to listen to the gospel in its entirety in ways convenient to them.

Many people, I suppose, put the unsolicited circular CD into their circular file as soon as they received it. A few, however, heeded my request. Several of them told me that when they listened to the gospel story in long sections — even the whole gospel in its entirety — they realized that entire chapters and more were not just collections of individual stories but a narrative which had a beginning, a middle, and an end. They understood that many of the individual stories were connected to others in ways they had not realized, and when they got to the end they were shocked to hear the gospel conclude at the empty tomb without any resurrection appearances of Jesus.

Hearing the gospel as a whole in this way also helped me appreciate Mark anew. I began to realize more fully that he had not haphazardly slapped together a series of episodes about Jesus, but he had crafted a unified story in a way that the whole became greater than the sum of the individual parts. For example, when I heard the familiar parables of the kingdom of God immediately after, and in conjunction with, the story in which Jesus' family had come looking for him, I heard Mark saying something about Jesus' family which I hadn't heard before!

And when I heard Mark telling the women "he is going before you to Galilee, as he had told you; there you will see him," followed by them running away without telling anyone — ending the gospel without anyone seeing Jesus — I began to wonder exactly what "go to Galilee" might really mean. Had I missed an important part of the big picture?

Projection

Finally, there is the problem we might call projection. Too often we project upon the gospel writers the images of selfless saints without flaw or bias — gods in their own right, if you will — instead of seeing them as human beings who had agendas and points of view like other people. Furthermore, we project upon their gospels our own sets of beliefs and biases, hearing what we want to hear rather than listening to what they may really be saying. We often do the same with Jesus — projecting upon him what we want him to be.

When it comes to our reading of Mark, we must be careful that we focus on what Mark is saying — not on what we *want* him to say. A problem with this, of course, is that we may discover we don't like what he has to say.

We must also ask this question: Has Mark projected his own biases and points of view upon Jesus and created Jesus in his own image?

Chapter 4

Can We Trust Mark?

This brings us to the question of trust. Can we trust Mark? This may seem like an odd question to ask — especially at the beginning of a study. Trust is something that is established after you have gotten to know someone. How can we ask the question of trust before we have even started?

There are two parts to this question. The first is relatively easy to address. The second is more problematic.

Mark, the Document

The first is this: Can we trust Mark, the document? That is, can we trust that the document which we read in our modern translations today is actually the document that Mark wrote almost two millennia ago? After all, there is no surviving first edition of the gospel of Mark. We do not have an original manuscript. The oldest documents that contain even portions of the gospel date from the beginning of the third century, or about 170 years after the crucifixion. The oldest complete manuscripts are from the fourth century, or at least 270 years after Jesus.

Of course, if all of those documents agreed — that is, if they were exact copies without error or differences — there would be little disagreement as to what the "original" behind the copies might be. But these were not photocopies. Scribes may have painstakingly copied from originals, but mistakes in copying were inevitably made — and if a scribe was copying from a manuscript with a mistake, that mistake would invariably be passed on to others.

Furthermore, some of the manuscripts or fragments are written in Greek, but others are in Aramaic, Syriac, and Latin. Some, found mostly in letters, are short quotes of passages. Others are paraphrases that give a sense of a passage but not an exact translation. There are about 2,400 different documents containing at least portions of the gospels. All of this makes determining what an original Mark may have looked like a daunting task.

In addressing these concerns, scholars have catalogued all of the documents and variations that have been found. Then, when publishing editions of the Bible today, they have to choose which manuscripts they will follow, often showing in footnotes what variations they *haven't* chosen, so a reader can see what some alternate readings might be.

For example, the Greek New Testament on my desk is one published by the United Bible Societies. The editors of that book have judged various passages to be more or less "certain" using a letter system from "A" to "D." Passages marked with an "A" are deemed to be "virtually certain." "B" means there is some doubt as to whether a reading can be called certain. "C" means there is considerable doubt, and "D" indicates a high amount of doubt as to the certainty of a text. We will visit one way they decide what is "doubtful" below.

Brackets [ ] are also used when the editors believe words or passages are of "dubious textual validity," and double brackets [[   ]] are used when the editors believe the passage is a "later addition" which they have included either because of its antiquity or because they feel it adds some other value to the text.

Some of the textual variations are minor and don't change the meaning of the passage or the intent of the author. Others are more significant. For example, the New Revised Standard Version (NRSV) of the gospel of

Mark begins this way:

1. The beginning of the good news of Jesus Christ, the Son of God[1]
2. As it is written in the prophet Isaiah[2]...

As you can see, the NRSV editors have added a footnote to each verse. The footnote to verse one reads "other ancient manuscripts lack *the Son of God*." The footnote to verse 2 reads "other ancient manuscripts read *in the prophets*" (rather than "in the prophet Isaiah").

Taking the second verse first, the difference of the meaning of the words "in the prophet Isaiah" versus "in the prophets" is of little consequence as to the meaning and intent of Mark. Furthermore, the editors of my Greek New Testament give an "A" to the certainty of the use of the words "in the prophet Isaiah." Based upon their study of the ancient manuscripts, they are confident that this reading is "certain."

There is less confidence regarding the first verse, however, although you wouldn't know it from reading the NRSV footnote. This is where consulting the Greek edition of the New Testament proves helpful, for the editors of that book give more information. They put the words "the son of God" in brackets, indicating that they believe these words to be of "dubious textual validity," and they use a "C" rather than an "A" as to the certainty of the text.

In other words, their study of the ancient manuscripts has led them to conclude that there is "considerable doubt" as to whether Mark used the words "Son of God" in the first line of his gospel. This is of much more significance!

Since some of the ancient manuscripts include this verse, and others do not, how do scholars determine which one is more likely to have been written by Mark? Not which one do they like better, but which one did Mark more likely write?

Among other things, when there is doubt as to the certainty of a passage, one question asked is this:

> "Based upon the integrity of the manuscript, the context of the passage, and what we know of the author, is it more likely that the author would have included these words in this place and a later copyist deleted them,
>
> OR
>
> is it more likely that the author did **not** include them, and they were added by a later copyist?"

In the case of the first verse of Mark, the questions might be put this way:

> "Is it more likely that Mark would have included the words 'Son of God' in the first verse, and some later copyist/editor took them out,
>
> OR
>
> is it more likely that Mark did **not** include them in the first verse, and that someone added them later?"

The answer to the above question is made easier by the simple fact that the oldest manuscripts don't include these words. For this reason alone, one might conclude that Mark did not originally write them. Furthermore, it seems more likely that someone would have added words like these if they weren't already there, than that someone would have removed them if they were. The general consensus is that these words are a later addition, which is the reason the editors of my Greek New Testament give this variant a "C" instead of an "A" — which is not to say that Mark didn't believe Jesus to be the Son of God. After all, Mark brings his gospel to a climax as the centurion beneath the cross calls Jesus "God's Son" (the only human being to make this claim in Mark's gospel, by the way). However, whether Mark intended to *start* his gospel by announcing that Jesus is the Son of God is uncertain.

Of course, the lack of the words "Son of God" in this verse doesn't change the overall meaning of the gospel. Furthermore, the vast majority of the textual variations in Mark are like this and don't affect the overall meaning of the text. In fact, of the 161 words or phrases that are given letter grades in my Greek New Testament, only eight are given a grade of "D" — and most of those eight have to do with concerns such as to whether a preposition or possessive pronoun is to be used or not.

The bottom line is this: because of the rigorous work of textual scholars, we can be confident as to the integrity of the text that is before us. We can trust Mark, the document. Which English translation you use, however, is another matter (more on this in the next chapter).

Mark the Storyteller and Theologian

Can we trust Mark the theologian and storyteller? This is more difficult to assess and determine. How can we, from this distance, discern whether what Mark is telling us is true or not? Can we be sure that what Mark records is what really happened? Did he correctly understand and transmit what Jesus actually said and did? Is it possible that he includes stories that were attributed to Jesus or were said to be about Jesus, but were actually done or said by someone else? And when Mark summarizes or makes a side comment, does he correctly interpret what was said?

Can we trust *Mark*?

One thing we know is this: both Matthew and Luke trusted Mark enough to use his gospel as the starting point for their own. By and large, they have included what Mark has written within their own gospels, often in the same order he presented it and sometimes word for word. This is another way we can affirm the integrity of the text of Mark. When they do make changes, it is often to use words of their own liking or in order to clarify or expand upon something being reported. Where Mark uses the term "kingdom of God," for example, Matthew prefers the term "kingdom of heaven." Similarly, at the Transfiguration, when Mark reports that the voice from the cloud says "This is my beloved Son, listen to him," Luke leaves out the word "beloved" and adds "my chosen." Many of these changes don't significantly alter Mark's narrative, nor do they suggest any lack of trust in Mark by Matthew and Luke.

But they didn't trust him entirely.

For one thing, they both agree that Mark hasn't told the whole story. They add material to which Mark may not have had access or that Mark may have intentionally left out such as the lineage of Jesus and infancy narratives.

At other times they leave out something that Mark has included. They both omit, for example, the miracle of the healing of the blind man of Bethsaida (Mark 8:22-26), perhaps because it displays some magical elements with which they may not have been comfortable or because Matthew and Luke thought it to be a commentary by Mark on the blindness of the disciples.

And they certainly don't agree with Mark's account of the discovery of the empty tomb and what follows. When Luke, for example, comes to the end of Mark's gospel and discovers no resurrection appearances of Jesus, what does Luke do? He adds another witness! Instead of saying that there was just one man at the tomb, he says there were two. He then adds several stories of appearances of Jesus. It's as if he is saying "Mark wasn't the only witness to the resurrection. Here is the real story!" As for Matthew, he not only turns one witness into two, he calls them "angels" (a term Luke later uses when Cleopas is speaking with the "stranger" on the road to Emmaus).

However, I believe that both Matthew and Luke have misread and misunderstood — or if they did understand they disagreed and chose to change — what Mark had to say. Just because Mark doesn't have resurrection appearances where we expect them to be, for example, doesn't mean he has omitted them. As we shall see, when we read Mark the way he wants to be read, we will find him to be a very trustworthy witness, indeed.

Chapter 5

Principles for Reading the Gospels

Before proceeding, it will be helpful to review a few basic principles which may help us understand Mark (and all the gospels):

1) The gospels are summary documents, not verbatim accounts;
2) The gospels are documents of interpretation and translation, even at their earliest stage; and
3) Theology trumps chronology (even when it comes to the resurrection).

Principle One:
The Gospels Are Summary Documents, not Verbatim Accounts

A first principle in reading Mark, I believe, is to understand the "summary" nature of his presentation. Mark was not a court stenographer. He did not have a tape recorder or video camera. He did not have an opportunity to record, word for word, everything that Jesus said or did. In many instances, he had to put into his own words the message that Jesus was imparting.

Consider the first words of Jesus as recorded by Mark. They come after the appearance of John the Baptist, after the baptism of Jesus, and after Jesus has gone into the wilderness:

> Now after John was arrested, Jesus came to Galilee, proclaiming the good news of God, and saying "The time is fulfilled,

and the kingdom of God has come near; repent and believe in the good news."
— Mark 1:14-15

We can be sure, of course, that these nineteen words were not the only words Jesus spoke as he walked from place to place. He didn't mindlessly say them over and over again, for example, as people passed by — like a replaying video in a department store shopping aisle — nor did he stand on a street corner with a sandwich board emblazoned with these words.

But we can't be sure that these are Jesus' exact words. There is no contemporaneous record of what Jesus said when he first appeared, or at any other point of his ministry, for that matter.

Rather, Mark is recording what we might call a "summary statement" of Jesus' message as he understood it — the gist of what Jesus was saying, if you will. The words "the kingdom of God has come near; repent and believe in the good news" might even be called the title of Jesus' first sermon, not the whole text. Mark fills in the text later in the gospel — in the section with the parables of the kingdom of God, for example — but in order to prepare the way he begins by giving us a summary of Jesus' message.

Does this mean that these words are Mark's creation and not authentic words of Jesus? Not at all. Whether Jesus said these exact words or whether they are Mark's summary of what Jesus said does not detract from their authenticity. If they communicate the gist of what Jesus was saying, they are for us the authentic message of Jesus.

Of course, even if we had a contemporaneous record of what Jesus had said when he first appeared, we still could not be sure that the reporter had recorded exact words. This became clear to me when I bought two area newspapers that were published on the same day and compared the different ways the sports writers of these papers reported a baseball game from the previous night. Both writers saw the same game. Both reported the same final score. But both reported in their own style and highlighted different aspects of the game. One extensively quoted the manager of the home team. The other didn't quote him at all. Interestingly, both newspapers quoted one specific ballplayer, but the quotes were not identical. I have placed the quotes below, one after the other, for comparison:

> I think when these West Coast teams came into Shea, they came a little lackadaisical. I think they know now they're going to be in for a good game.
> *Star-Ledger*

> Every team we play now comes in against us a little lax. Now they know we have a good ball club. They have to break their neck to win against us.
> *The Record*

Both writers were quoting the same player, on the same night, in the same locker room. They both got the gist of what the player said. But even in this age of videotape and tape recorders, both quoted him rather differently.

Similarly, we can assume that the gospel stories are summary, not verbatim, reports — but if they give us the gist of what Jesus had said or done as they understood it, we can consider them to be accurate and authentic accounts.

This is also true when it comes to the crafting of speeches. We can assume that Mark and the other gospel writers took what they knew of Jesus and his teaching and strung together longer narratives or speeches in order that the material might make sense and have meaning for them and their contemporaries.

We do something similar when retelling our own history even today. For example, in the Broadway play 1776 the authors used words and music to express what the founding fathers of the United States said and did. They drew upon primary documents and accounts of what happened, and used much of what the characters actually said and wrote. However, in putting together a script, they had to create dialogue and telescope events in such a way as to make sense of the issues and fit the action within the parameters of a play. Without always being literally correct, they expressed the gist of the story as they understood it and in a way that would speak to people living 200 years after the fact — although surely Franklin, Adams, Jefferson, and others did not sing and dance their way up and down the steps of Independence Hall!

We can be sure that Mark and the other gospel writers took what they knew of the words and events of the life of Jesus and fashioned and re-fashioned them in ways that spoke to their generation. In so doing, they stood in good biblical company. The authors of Deuteronomy, for example, had done the same when they penned the speeches of Moses, crafting what they believed Moses would have said to the generations alive after the settling of the promised land, who lived in cities they "had not built" (Deuteronomy 6:10ff).

In our generation, the question "What would Jesus do?" has gained popularity. Mark, Luke, and the others asked a similar question, except they rephrased it with the words "What would Jesus say? What would he say to our generation, if he were here? Knowing who Jesus was and is, what would he say to us?" It's a question we still ask.

Principle Two:
The Gospels Are Documents of Interpretation and Translation, Even at the Earliest Stages

A complicating factor in understanding the gospel of Mark (and the other gospels) is a problem of translation. For one thing, the language of Jesus and his disciples was Aramaic, which was the common language of the people of Israel in Jesus' day. The oldest manuscripts we have of Mark, however, are written in Greek, the *lingua franca* of the ancient world. The ancient writers knew that if you wanted the wider world to read your work, it had to be written in Greek. When putting it in Greek, Mark had to choose which words to use to best express the meaning of the Aramaic. In so doing he was not just translating. He was putting someone else's words and ideas into his own and thereby interpreting the meaning for others. For example, did Jesus actually say "those who lose their life... will save it" (Mark 8:35) or did he rather say "those who hate their life... will keep it" (John 12:25)? I must say I prefer Mark's way of putting it, but it is possible that both John and Mark were translating the same saying Jesus originally said in Aramaic and putting it into their own words in Greek.

The same thing happens when we read in English what has been translated from the Greek. Different English translations use different words and phrases to translate the same Greek passage. Some are more literal in their rendering of the Greek and rely on footnotes for explanation. Others are paraphrases and use modern idioms to get at the meaning of a passage. Whichever your preference may be, it is often helpful to consult more than one translation in order to get a better sense of the author's intent. In this study we will generally follow the

New Revised Standard Version, but will also consult the "original" Greek in order to consider alternate ways the text might be rendered.

In addition, we will look at the ways Luke and Matthew followed and/or changed Mark when they wrote their "translations" of his gospel — which brings us back to the example of the baseball player being quoted by two different writers. When comparing what Matthew, Mark, and Luke wrote, we must remember that they are not three reporters who are quoting Jesus. Rather, if Mark wrote first, and if Matthew and Luke had Mark in front of them when they wrote, it is Matthew and Luke who are the reporters quoting what Mark has written about Jesus. The way they *changed* Mark will give us insight into how they interpreted what he had written, as well as give us an understanding as to what biases they believe Mark may have had (and give us an insight into biases of their own).

Principle Three:
Theology Trumps Chronology, Even When It Comes to the Resurrection!

A third concern in reading the gospel accounts has to do with the order of the narrative.

Mark, for example, tells us that Jesus didn't begin his public ministry until after John was put into prison. "Now after John was arrested, Jesus came to Galilee, proclaiming the good news of God..." (Mark 1:14).

The gospel of John, on the other hand, reports that Jesus began his public ministry *before* John was imprisoned. "John, of course, had not yet been thrown into prison" (John 3:24).

Which is correct?

Consider that in Mark the only recorded visits of Jesus to Jerusalem occur during what we now call Holy Week (Mark 11:1ff). It is during this final week that Mark reports Jesus overturning the tables of the money changers.

John, on the other hand, reported several visits of Jesus to Jerusalem over the course of several years — and the overturning of the tables in the temple comes at the beginning of Jesus' public ministry rather than the end (John 2:13ff).

Which is correct?

The truth is, we really don't know and the gospel writers probably didn't know, either.

Except for the crucifixion and resurrection itself, it's probable that none of the gospel writers knew exactly *when* various events of Jesus' public ministry occurred. Since Mark crafted his story in such a way that he reported only one visit to Jerusalem, he had to place the overturning of the tables during that visit. Since John reported several visits, it makes sense that Jesus would do it the first time he appeared at the temple — and there are strong theological reasons for placing it at the beginning, even if exactly when it happened is unknown.

The basic question facing Mark and the other gospel writers who recorded the events and the meaning of Jesus' life and ministry was this: "How should we tell the stories?" In what order should they be put to emphasize the points they were trying to make? Should they put the turning over of the tables in the temple at the beginning or the end of Jesus' ministry? Should Jesus' appellation of Peter as "the rock" come at the beginning or in the middle? Exactly when, in relation to his total ministry, did the stilling of the storm occur, the feeding of the 5,000, or the institution of what we now call the Lord's Supper?

Mark, it would seem, chose a path that began with the baptism of Jesus and the call of the first disciples. He then depicted a typical day in the life of Jesus, followed by various episodes that he grouped according to theme rather than chronology, in order to emphasize the points he wanted to make. He interspersed three passion predictions through his narrative and concluded with one visit to Jerusalem. And he chose not to put any post-resurrection appearances of Jesus following the story of the empty tomb.

However, if theology trumps chronology, we must consider the possibility that even resurrection appearances can be repositioned, just as can any other episode. In fact, we know that this happened in other gospels. Consider, for example, the story of the miraculous catch of fish reported by both Luke and John. In both gospels, the story is a call to leave fishing and follow Jesus. Luke, however, included it as a miracle at the *beginning* of Jesus' ministry. John, on the other hand, placed it as a resurrection appearance at the *end* of Jesus' ministry. Which was it? Is it a miracle story John misplaced after the resurrection, or a resurrection appearance Luke misplaced before the resurrection? Whichever it was, we can see that unless it happened twice, at least one of the gospel writers has "misplaced" it in an instance of theology trumping chronology.

This, as we shall see, is something that Mark does very well, particularly when it comes to the resurrection.

Chapter 6

Go to Galilee:
The Resurrection in Mark

When Mark related the events and conversations of the night before Jesus died, among other things he reported that Jesus told his disciples he would go to Galilee ahead of them after he is raised (Mark 14:28). These words are echoed by the young man inside the empty tomb (Mark 16:7).

When I first heard these words, I assumed that Jesus meant he was going to the *geographic* region of Galilee, where he had conducted his ministry. It seems that Matthew, the only synoptic gospel to record a post-resurrection appearance of Jesus in Galilee, assumed this, as well.

Luke, however, would have none of that. When he reported the episode in which Jesus predicted Peter's denial, Luke omitted Jesus' words that he would go to Galilee. Neither was this message uttered at the empty tomb. Instead, Luke's post-resurrection stories center in and around Jerusalem. His first reported appearance of Jesus, for example, is to Cleopas (of whom we'll hear more later) and another, unnamed, disciple on the road a few miles outside Jerusalem. Luke also reported that Jesus appeared on Easter Day to Peter. Later that evening, Jesus appears to "the eleven and their companions" announcing that the message of repentance and forgiveness is to be proclaimed not from Galilee but "beginning from Jerusalem" (Luke 24:47). Finally, Luke's story of the ascension of Jesus (the only gospel writer to report it), occurred in nearby Bethany, with the disciples then returning to Jerusalem

(Luke 24:50ff). The fact is that Luke did not report any appearances of Jesus in Galilee, nor did the disciples go there for any reason.

Of course, when it comes to resurrection appearances of Jesus in Galilee, it seems that Mark would have none of that, either, for even though he told the disciples to go to Galilee in order to see Jesus, he doesn't actually report any post-empty tomb appearances of Jesus in Galilee, or anywhere else, for that matter.

Why would Mark announce that Jesus had risen, tell people to go to Galilee in order to see him, and then fail to report any resurrection appearances, especially with such a strong tradition affirming those appearances? We can assume that Mark was aware of that tradition, as it is a tradition which Paul — writing before Mark — referred to when he recorded what was undoubtedly one of the earliest of Christian creeds:

> For I handed on to you as of first importance what I in turn had received: that Christ died for our sins in accordance with the scriptures, and that he was buried, and that he was raised on the third day in accordance with the scriptures, and that he appeared to Cephas, then to the twelve. Then he appeared to more than 500 brothers and sisters at one time, most of whom are still alive, though some have died. Then he appeared to James, then to all the apostles.
> — 1 Corinthians 15:3-7

Even so, Mark reported no appearances after the story of the empty tomb. Why?

The answer, I believe, may be found in the words "Go to Galilee."

Since Mark reported that people were told to go to Galilee to see Jesus, but then reported no sightings, could it be that the words "go to Galilee" have another meaning? Craftsman that he was, Mark may not have been saying "go to the literal region of Galilee where Jesus had his ministry" but rather "go back to the Galilee where you first met Jesus — in the gospel that you are reading! Go back to the beginning of the gospel. Read it again. There you will see him! There you will see the risen Christ!"

This meaning is confirmed, I believe, when we "go to Galilee" in this way and discover that Mark — in a quintessential example of theology trumping chronology — had placed three resurrection appearances within the body of the gospel, *before* the resurrection, "hidden in plain sight":

• The stilling of the storm (Mark 4:35-41)
• The walking on the water (Mark 6:47-52)
• The Transfiguration (Mark 9:2-8)

Although these episodes are normally catalogued among the miracles of Jesus, it is important to note significant differences between these stories and the other miracles — especially the language Mark used in the telling of these stories and his description of the reactions of the disciples to these episodes.

Let's take a closer look.

Chapter 7

Hidden in Plain Sight: Mark's Resurrection Stories

Mark set the stage for weaving the resurrection appearances into his gospel with an episode in his very first chapter which subtly prefigures the story of the empty tomb. It occurs in Capernaum on the day after the sabbath:

> In the morning, while it was still very dark, he got up and went out to a deserted place, and there he prayed. And Simon and his companions hunted for him. When they found him, they said to him, "Everyone is searching for you." He answered, "Let us go on to the neighboring towns, so that I may proclaim the message there also, for that is what I came out to do."
> — Mark 1:35ff

In this story, Mark prefigured the events of Easter Day:

- The episode began "in the morning, while it was still very dark," on the day after the sabbath. It is worth noting that Easter was also the day after the sabbath, and that early in the morning on that first Easter Day it was still very dark (in more ways than one).
- When Mark reported that Jesus "got up," he used the Greek word, *anistemi* — the same word Jesus would later use three times when he predicted that he would "arise."
- At dawn, Jesus would be missing — just as on Easter morning.
- Simon and others would go looking for him.

- When they found him, he told them "for that is what I came out (of the tomb?) to do."

The connection of this episode with the resurrection might be missed the first time someone reads the gospel. However, when we "go to Galilee" a second time and re-read the gospel — this time in the light of the resurrection — we understand what Mark is telling us in a new way. The first time, we hear Jesus, as a yet unknown preacher calling the disciples to follow him. The second time, we hear the same message — but now from the resurrected Lord! The one who arose is telling the disciples — and by extension, us — that the message "the kingdom of God is at hand, repent and believe the gospel," must be proclaimed *after* the resurrection just as it had been before the resurrection!

This "resurrection connection" imagery is found throughout Mark's gospel, but no stronger than in three stories that might be called "resurrection appearances" *before* the resurrection.

The Stilling of the Storm (Mark 4:35-41)
The first of these episodes comes at the end of chapter 4, often called the miracle of "the stilling of the storm." During the day, Jesus had been teaching a crowd about the nature of the kingdom of God while sitting in a boat by the shore of the Sea of Galilee. Mark then reported the following story:

> On that day, when evening had come, he said to them, "Let us go across to the other side." And leaving the crowd behind, they took him with them in the boat, just as he was. Other boats were with him. A great windstorm arose, and the waves beat into the boat, so that the boat was already being swamped. But he was in the stern, asleep on the cushion; and they woke him up and said to him, "Teacher, do you

not care that we are perishing?" He woke up and rebuked the wind, and said to the sea, "Peace! Be still!" Then the wind ceased, and there was a dead calm. He said to them, "Why are you afraid? Have you still no faith?" And they were filled with great awe and said to one another, "Who then is this, that even the wind and the sea obey him?"

A close reading of this passage reveals that it is no "mere" miracle story. Let's take it verse by verse:

On that day, when evening had come, he said to them, "Let us go across to the other side."

Most sailing expeditions would not begin as night was falling. This is an indication that this story may not really be about sailing, but about going to the "other side."

Furthermore, "that day" on which this episode occurs is a day on which Jesus has taught about the kingdom of God, indicating that Mark saw a connection between teaching about the kingdom and the storm that is to follow. Can it be a coincidence that on the night before Jesus died, Mark reported that Jesus had also been talking about the kingdom, saying: "I will never again drink of the fruit of the vine until that day I drink it new in the kingdom of God" (Mark 14:25)?

Jesus also was buried "when evening had come."

And leaving the crowd behind, they took him with them in the boat, just as he was.

After Jesus had died on the cross, there was no time for anointing his body for burial. He had been placed in the tomb quickly, "just as he was."

Other boats were with him.

It would be superfluous to mention other boats unless they represented something significant — perhaps people other than the disciples who were among those who followed Jesus, especially those who were mentioned in the stories of the crucifixion and resurrection. These others may have included people such as the women and Joseph of Arimathea.

> And a great windstorm arose, and the waves beat into the boat, so that the boat was already being swamped.

During the "windstorm" that was the arrest and crucifixion of Jesus, the "boat" which was the community of Jesus' followers was being "swamped." The twelve were overwhelmed with fear, and "all of them deserted him and fled" (Mark 14:50). Peter had denied him and wept during the trial (Mark 14:72). None of them were to be found at the crucifixion.

> But he was in the stern, asleep on the cushion.

The word rendered here as "asleep" (*katheudo*) is a word that can also be translated as "dead."

> And they woke him up...

The Greek word *egertheis*, rendered here as "woke up," is the same word used in the story of the empty tomb when the young man says to the women "he has been raised."

> ... and said to him, "Teacher, do you not care that we are perishing?" He woke up and rebuked the wind, and said to the sea "Peace! Be still!" Then the wind ceased, and there was a dead calm. He said to them "Why are you afraid?"

The words "Why are you afraid" echo the first words the young man says to the women at the empty tomb: "Do not be afraid." These words, along with the word "Peace," are the first words spoken to anyone who sees Jesus after the resurrection in the other gospels. Mark used them here to the same effect. That is another indication that this is a "resurrection appearance" story. We shall see these words again in the story when Jesus walked on the water.

"Have you no faith?"

This is perhaps the most obvious clue that this is not a story about sailing on the sea but about dealing with matters of faith, and it is made more profound and powerful when we realize that it is delivered by the risen Christ.

And they were filled with great awe and said to one another, "Who is this, that even the wind and the sea obey him?"

Mark, of course, knew who he was: He was the risen Lord!

Jesus Walks on Water (Mark 6:47-52)

Mark's second "resurrection appearance" story comes at the end of chapter 6, in the episode often called "Jesus walks on the water." Like the story of the stilling of the storm, the context of this passage is as important as the episode itself. It comes immediately following the miracle of the feeding of the 5,000. In that feeding story, Jesus had invited the disciples to go with him to a "deserted place" (eremon topon, the same words and imagery as in the resurrection connection story of chapter 1). The crowds followed, so Jesus decided to teach them until it was very late, at which point he directed the disciples to feed them. After the disciples produced but five loaves and two fishes, Jesus took the loaves, looked up to heaven, blessed and broke the loaves, and gave them to his disciples to distribute. He divided the fish in the same way. Five thousand people were fed, and twelve baskets of leftovers were gathered. After the feeding, Jesus sent the disciples across the lake in a boat, and after saying farewell to the crowd, he went up a hill alone to pray. Mark then told the story of the appearance of Jesus on the water:

> When evening came, the boat was out on the sea, and he was alone on the land. When he saw that they were straining at the oars, against an adverse wind, he came toward them early in the morning, walking on the sea. He intended to pass them by. But when they saw him walking on the sea, they thought it was a ghost and cried out, for they all saw him and were terrified. But immediately he spoke to them and said "Take heart, it is I. Do not be afraid!" Then he got into the boat with them, and the wind ceased. And they were utterly astounded, for **they did not understand about the loaves** (emphasis mine), but their hearts were hardened.

It's a wonderful story — but the final sentence seems odd. We would think the disciples would be astounded because Jesus had just walked on water! Instead, Mark says that they were astounded because "they did not understand about the loaves." With these words, Mark connected the story of the walking on the water to the miracle of the feeding of the 5,000, and in so doing he presented the events of Holy Thursday, Good Friday, and Easter Day:

• The feeding of the 5,000 was a Eucharistic meal, similar to the one the disciples shared with Jesus the night before he died.

- After the meal, the crowds and the disciples left Jesus, who prayed alone "on a hill" (Mount of Olives).
- Jesus then appeared to them in a way no living being could — walking on the water — and they thought it was a ghost, as if he was dead — which is what they actually thought after the crucifixion.
- Finally, Jesus spoke the words that accompany virtually every resurrection episode, "Do not be afraid," and the end of the story found the disciples confused and not understanding the real significance of what had just occurred.

The Transfiguration (Mark 9:2-8)

The story of the Transfiguration of Jesus is perhaps the clearest example of a resurrection appearance before the resurrection:

> Six days later, Jesus took with him Peter and James and John, and led them up a high mountain apart, by themselves. And he was transfigured before them, and his clothes became dazzling white, such as no one on earth could bleach them. And there appeared to them Elijah with Moses, who were talking with Jesus. Then Peter said to Jesus, "Rabbi, it is good for us to be here; let us make three dwellings, one for you, one for Moses, and one for Elijah." He did not know what to say, for they were terrified. Then a cloud overshadowed them, and from the cloud there came a voice, "This is my Son, the Beloved; listen to him!" Suddenly when they looked around, they saw no one with them any more, but only Jesus.

As far as context goes, this episode comes at a turning point in Mark's story. In the previous chapter, Peter made his confession of Jesus as the Messiah, and Jesus made the first of his three passion predictions. Craftsman that Mark was, he reported that Jesus told the disciples three times of his coming death and resurrection, balanced by three resurrection appearances of Jesus woven into his gospel. In this episode on the mountaintop, Mark plainly said that the disciples saw Jesus "transfigured" (changed) before them, and "his clothes became dazzling white, such as no one on earth could bleach them." Here is Jesus in his resurrected glory — before the resurrection!

As in the other appearance stories (and as opposed to other miracles of Jesus), the disciples were confused and afraid. Mark told us it came six days after the realization that Jesus was the messiah. This may also be Mark's way of saying that it happened six days after the resurrection. Furthermore, since it is the third and last of the appearance stories, and occurs on a mountaintop rather than the water, it is possible that this is Mark's version of the ascension of Jesus.

Extraordinary Miracles — or Misplaced Appearances?

The episodes known as the stilling of the storm, the walking on the water, and the Transfiguration are usually catalogued as miracles of Jesus which occurred during his lifetime, rather than as resurrection appearances which Mark has somehow placed — or misplaced — within his gospel. However, there are several elements in these episodes which separate them from other miracles of Jesus. For one thing, except for the miraculous feedings (that are connected to the appearance stories) virtually all of the miracles in Mark's gospel except these three have to do with healings of one sort or another. The reaction to the healing miracles is not fear but joy and amazement, and the fact that Jesus is seen as a *thaumaturge* (a holy man who is a practitioner of healing arts) is not considered unusual or in question.

In the stories of the stilling of the storm, the walking on the water, and the Transfiguration, however, the disciples were not joyful. Rather, they were filled with fear, disbelief, and confusion. Furthermore, these episodes occurred only in the presence of the disciples and other close followers of Jesus (as do the resurrection appearances themselves in the other gospels), whereas the healing miracles occurred in the presence or sight of others. Finally, these three stories were told in such a way that connected them with the resurrection and in which we see glimpses of the resurrected Lord, making them qualitatively different from the stories of healings.

In the absence of appearances of Jesus *after* the resurrection, is it possible to conclude that these episodes — which were not miracles of healing — were stories of resurrection appearances which Mark placed *before* the resurrection? If Mark wanted to make a theological point about the nature of Jesus — that Jesus was, for example, the resurrected Lord from the very beginning, not only after the resurrection but also before it (akin to how the gospel of John told us that Jesus existed before his appearance in human flesh as the eternal *logos*) — a creative way to do that might be to place the resurrection appearances themselves before the resurrection. This explanation especially appealed to the English literature major in me. It revealed the artistry of Mark as an author who used a subtle and literary way to express a theological truth about the nature of Jesus and who he was.

Mission Accomplished?

I would have ended my study with that — "Mark is the resurrection gospel in which he presented Jesus as the resurrected Lord from the start" — except for one little thing: that pesky last line of his story!

> So they went out and fled from the tomb, for terror and amazement had seized them, and they said nothing to any one, for they were afraid.
> — Mark 16:8

If Mark was only trying to make the point that Jesus was the resurrected Lord, even before the resurrection, why not just end at verse 7?

> But go, tell his disciples and Peter that he is going ahead of you to Galilee; there you will see him, just as he told you.
> — Mark 16:7

This would be the perfect way to end, with forward-looking words of anticipation and hope of seeing the risen Lord, whether in geographic or literary Galilee.

However, Mark doesn't do that. Instead, after telling the women to tell Peter and the other disciples to go to Galilee, Mark reported that they ran away and didn't say anything to anyone! Here was the greatest news these women or anyone else had ever heard — news Mark would want shouted from housetops — yet he ended his gospel with the words "they said nothing to anyone..."

Is something else, beyond or in addition to chronology or theology, going on here?

Another Possibility: Politics

As much as we might want to believe "there are no politics in church," we know that's not the case. Wherever there are people, there will be issues about which they will disagree and over which they will take sides — even in the church. This is true of the church today, and it was true of the early church as well. Issues about which those in the early church disagreed included theological concerns such as "is salvation through works or faith," and "is it proper to eat food sacrificed to idols?" They also included more mundane matters such as who should serve at table and how to wear one's hair. And they included leadership issues and (dare we care them political?) divisions.

Paul tells us as much in his first letter to the church in Corinth:

> Now I appeal to you, brothers and sisters, by the name of our Lord Jesus Christ, that all of you be in agreement and that there be no divisions among you, but that you be united in the same mind and the same purpose. For it has been reported to me by Chloe's people that there are quarrels among you, my brothers and sisters. What I mean is that each of you says, "I belong to Paul," or "I belong to Apollos," or "I belong to Cephas," or "I belong to Christ." Has Christ been divided?
> — 1 Corinthians 1:10-13a

The verb translated as "divided" in verse 13 (*merizo*) is related to the common term for the Greek word for "party." Paul, in essence, is asking if the church has been divided into "political parties."

What about Mark? He did not write in a vacuum. If he wrote in part to address issues and concerns that were facing the early church, it is probable that he was aligned with one group or another within the early church.

Of which group was he a part? To which "party" did he belong — *and did his omission of appearances of Jesus after the story of the empty tomb have anything to do with his alignment?*

In order to try to answer those questions, let's take a closer look at who Mark may have been.

Chapter 8

Who Was Mark?

Although the gospel is called "the gospel according to Mark," it is only in the title that the name appears. He is not listed as one of the twelve disciples. There is no character in the story called Mark. No contemporary writer refers to him by name.

Who, then, was Mark?

The short answer is, of course, "We really don't know."

But there is a longer answer.

Early Church Tradition

Papias, a bishop of Hierapolis in south central Turkey around AD 150, is quoted by the early church historian Eusebius as saying that the author of the gospel of Mark was a companion to and "interpreter of" Peter.

It's possible that Papias came to this conclusion because the letter of 1 Peter mentions someone named Mark who was with Peter in Rome — and whom Peter also called his "son." Unfortunately, many people shared the same name (think of all of the people named "John" or "Mary" in the New Testament). The fact that someone named Mark may have at one time accompanied Peter — or even if Peter had a son (if only a son in the faith) by that name — does not mean he is the Mark who wrote the gospel of that name.

However, Papias' assertion may have been influenced as much by *theology* as by anything else. What I mean is this: It was very important to the early church that the documents which we now call scripture be "apostolic," that is, they either had to be written by an apostle or by someone who was a contemporary of and who knew the apostles. For the gospel of Mark to be included in the canon, it needed an apostolic connection. Papias gives it that connection.

More significantly, however, is the fact that the gospel itself does not read as if it were written by someone who was close to Peter. At the least, we would expect an account of an appearance of Jesus to Peter after the resurrection!

This is not to say that the Mark who wrote the gospel did not know Peter or did not live during the apostolic age. We will just have to look in other places for corroboration.

Mark in the Book of Acts

One place to look is in the book of Acts, written by Luke. Since Luke wrote after Mark and had Mark's gospel in front of him when he wrote, it is possible that he may have known Mark personally — or known of him — and may have included him in his accounts. There are a few hints that this may have been the case.

One hint is found in Acts 12. In that passage Luke reported that Peter, after a miraculous release from prison in Jerusalem, went to "the house of Mary, the mother of John, whose other name was Mark..." (Acts 12:12). If this "John Mark" also lived in Jerusalem, or had visited his mother there during the time of the Passover when Jesus was crucified, it is possible that he himself had seen Jesus and was an eyewitness to the events of Holy Week. It also suggests a connection of Mark with Peter shortly after the resurrection.

But was that John Mark a *companion* to Peter? Luke does not so indicate. Rather, Luke tells us in Acts 12:25 that this Mark became an assistant to Paul and Barnabas and accompanied them from Syrian Antioch to the island of Cyprus. When Paul and his companions set sail from Cyprus and went to Perga in Asia Minor, however, John Mark "left them and returned to Jerusalem" (Acts 13:13).

Why John Mark went back to Jerusalem was not made clear by Luke. It is interesting to note that it came immediately after Paul had blinded a Jewish magician named Elymas. It may be that John Mark was not happy about that incident and went to Jerusalem to report on Paul to the leadership there (Jesus, after all, gave sight to the blind — he didn't blind the seeing). On the other hand, John Mark may have returned to Jerusalem for some other reason — to see his mother, for example. Whatever the reason, Paul was not happy about it. This was made clear later, when John Mark showed up again in Syrian Antioch upon Paul's return. Paul was ready to start another missionary journey, and Barnabas wanted to take John Mark along with them once again. Paul, however, stated that he did not want to take someone who had "deserted" them earlier (Acts 15:36-38).

At this point, Barnabas — who had once befriended and stood by Paul when Paul was not trusted by the church — now stood by Mark instead of Paul. His opposition to Paul was so extreme that he and Paul parted company and went their separate ways — Paul with Silas to Syria and Cilicia, and Barnabas with John Mark back to Cyprus. (Luke had told us earlier that Barnabas — who he called a Levite originally named Joseph — was a native of Cyprus.) After this, Luke never mentioned Barnabas or John Mark again.

Mark in Paul's Letters
The name Mark appears several times in Paul's letters. The only real information we glean, however, is found in Colossians, where Paul called someone named Mark

a "cousin of Barnabas" (Colossians 4:10). If this was the same Mark as the John Mark from the book of Acts, it may be one reason why Barnabas stood by him instead of Paul.

In any event, we have no evidence that this John Mark was either a companion to Peter or a member of the "party" of Paul.

Mark in Mark

Luke, Paul, and Papias, however, are not our only — or even primary — sources regarding Mark — if indeed he is the same person as the author of the gospel by that name. Rather, the best resource we have regarding the author of the gospel of Mark is the gospel itself.

Unfortunately, Mark nowhere in his gospel explicitly identifies himself, nor does he tell us how he came by his information about Jesus. We never read "I Mark, who was present in Galilee…" or "I, Mark, who collected these materials from eyewitnesses…." Neither did he tell us if he was among those who met Jesus on one of his journeys, or if he was present in Jerusalem during Holy Week.

Artist that he was, however, there are several intriguing passages in which he provides us some clues as to his identity.

One such passage comes in chapter 14, after Jesus is arrested in the Garden of Gethsemane. Mark reported that all of the disciples deserted Jesus and fled, but:

> …a certain young man was following him, wearing nothing but a linen cloth. They caught hold of him, but he left the linen cloth and ran off naked.
> — Mark 14:51-52

These verses seem oddly out of place. This enigmatic "young man" (*neaniskos* in the Greek) seems to come out of thin air, and then vanishes just as quickly, back into the air. He hadn't appeared in the story before. No name or other identification was given him.

Who is this "certain *neaniskos*," and why does he appear? Why would Mark — careful author I believe him to be — have included him in his gospel? Matthew and Luke left him out completely, by the way. Why mention him at all?

Back in my seminary class, my professor had suggested that this young man was Mark himself. He called these verses Mark's "signature," Mark's way of inserting himself into the story and revealing himself to his readers.

Other artists have done the same when creating their work. Nineteenth-century artist Winslow Homer, in his painting *The Veteran in a New Field*, placed his initials on a canteen located behind the character in the painting. French cyclorama artist Paul Philippoteaux painted himself into the action of Pickett's Charge in the Battle of Gettysburg (now on display in the National Military Park Museum and Visitor Center in Gettysburg, Pennsylvania). Director Alfred Hitchcock invariably placed himself as an extra in a scene in each of his films.

In a similar manner, Mark may have painted himself into the gospel picture by giving himself a cameo appearance in the scene in the Garden of Gethsemane. This, however, may not have been his only appearance in the gospel narrative, for the person who met the women outside the empty tomb on Easter morning was also an unnamed *neaniskos* — the only other time that Mark used that word in his gospel.

Could that also be Mark? If it was, those references may have been Mark's way of telling us that he was a witness to Holy Week. If we want to find other clues as to the identity of Mark, the accounts of that week would be a good place to start. First, however, we must turn to a group which Mark never mentioned by name, but whose influence pervaded his gospel.

The Essenes

Who are the Essenes? What do they have to do with Mark or Jesus?

The truth is, the Essenes (like Mark himself) are never mentioned by name in the gospel. For that reason, many of us don't know of them, nor would we even think to ask. However, the Essenes were an important part of the landscape of Judaism during the age in which Jesus lived. Much of what we know about them we learn from a contemporary of Mark named Josephus. Josephus was a Jewish general who led troops in a rebellion against Rome in AD 66. After the war he wrote several books which give not only accounts of the war but also the history leading up to the war, interspersed with notes about Jewish life and culture — including sections devoted to the Essenes. In his book *Bellum Judaeorum* (The Jewish War), written shortly after the end of the war, he named the Essenes as one of the three major sects of Judaism, along with the Pharisees and Sadducees. In another of his books, his autobiography *Vita*, he told us that he studied the ways of these sects when he was sixteen as he sought his own path in life. After spending three years in the desert with an ascetic named Barus, however, he decided to live as a Pharisee. Below is a summary, from *Bellum Judaeorum*, of some of what he has to say about the Essenes.[1]

1) Marriage and children: Many Essenes practiced celibacy and did not marry. Rather, they selected and taught other people's children, who themselves in turn became a part of the order. There was a second order of Essenes, however, that was like the first "in its way of life, customs, and rules," but differed only in that they permitted marriage.

2) Travel and attitudes toward strangers: Essenes were scattered throughout Israel and had "large colonies everywhere." When they traveled, they would carry "no baggage at all, but only weapons to keep off bandits." In every town a local Essene was assigned to look after strangers and to provide them with clothing and food. When strangers arrived, "all local resources" were made available to them, "as if they were their own," and the visitors would be hosted by people they had never seen before "as if they were old friends."

3) Medicine and healing: Essenes valued learning and studied "ancient writers." They were especially concerned with the healing arts, including the value of "medicinal roots and the properties of stones" in the treatment of illnesses.

4) Work and eating arrangements: Each Essene went to work each day "to the craft he understands best." At noon he would put on a "linen loincloth" and, after washing, would enter a house "which no one outside their community is allowed to enter." In the evening they would return and "take supper in the same way."

5) Attitude toward property: Josephus calls Essenes "communists"; that is, when someone joined the Essenes, they were expected to give all their property to the order. They continued working at a job like anyone else, but pooled their income with the group. No one individual owned anything but everything belonged to them all.

By now you may be asking yourself the question as to whether Jesus was — or ever had been — an Essene. Considering the way Josephus described them, there seems to be many points in Jesus' ministry that reflect the influence of an order like the Essenes:

1) **Marriage and children:** Jesus — who, like one order of the Essenes, did not marry — selected and taught other people's children. Although we often think of the disciples as grown men when Jesus called them (Mark 1:30 revealed that Simon Peter was old enough to have a mother-in-law) we really don't know how old any of them were. After all, when a boy or girl reached the age of puberty — as young as twelve and thirteen — he or she would be considered an adult, would work in professions (as even younger children would), would be given in marriage, and could go off to study with various teachers or schools (as Josephus did at the age of sixteen when he went to live with Barus). Some of Jesus' students (the word "disciple" can also be rendered as "student") may have been just this age.

2) **Travel and hospitality to strangers:** Consider what Mark reported when Jesus sent his disciples out in pairs:

> He ordered them to take nothing for their journey except a staff — no bread, no bag, no money in their belts, but to wear sandals and not to put on two tunics. He said to them "Wherever you enter a house, stay there until you leave the place."
> — Mark 6:8-10

The Essene practice of hosting strangers and sharing "all local resources" assured the disciples that they would be cared for as they went from town to town. It also revealed the kind of hospitality Mark described when Jesus, on what we now call Palm Sunday, sent his disciples to borrow the donkey upon which to enter the city, and later that week when he sends them to find a room in which to celebrate the Passover.

3) Medicine and healing: Jesus' early reputation was based, in part at least, on his healing powers, and several of the healings Mark described involve the kinds of practices Essenes may have learned in their study of the healing arts. These may have included the use of saliva and the placing of hands on the eyes of a blind man (Mark 8:22-25); spitting and touching the ears and tongue of a deaf-mute (Mark 7:33); and even the use of what might be called special incantations, to which Mark may refer by leaving certain words in Aramaic: *talitha koum*, which means "little girl get up" (Mark 5:41); and *ephphatha* which means "be opened" (Mark 7:34).

4) Eating arrangements: In Mark 3:31 Jesus' mother and brothers arrive at a house in which Jesus was to be found. If this was an Essene-like "building which others could not enter" it would explain why even Jesus' biological family must stand outside and send in a message to him.

5) Attitude toward property: The "communistic" lifestyle practiced by the Essenes was commended by Jesus to the rich man in Mark 10:21: "Sell all you have and give the money to the poor, and you will have riches in heaven; then come and follow me." Luke plainly said that this was the way the church in Jerusalem was organized after the resurrection in Acts 2:44-45, and Barnabas did just that — selling a field and laying the money "at the disciples' feet" — in Acts 4:37. Mark implied — if he did not say it plainly — that this was the way Jesus and his disciples lived, as well. "We have left everything and followed you" Peter said to Jesus (Mark 10:28), to which Jesus responded with words that suggested he and the disciples were part of an Essene-like network of communities:

> Truly I tell you, there is no one who has left house or brothers or sisters or mother or father or children or fields for my sake and the sake of the good news who will not receive a hundredfold now in this age — houses, brothers and sisters, mothers and children, and fields, with persecutions — and in the age to come eternal life.
> — Mark 10:29-30

It's important to note that Jesus told the rich man to give his wealth to "the poor." Does this refer to people living in actual poverty, or could it have other connotations?

Essenes and "the Poor"

Although Mark mentioned the Pharisees and Sadducees, the Herodians, the Romans, and even the Zealots, he never used the word "Essene." That doesn't mean, however, that Mark omitted them from his gospel, for in addition to the above indirect ways he referred to them by incorporating their customs and way of life into his narrative, he may also have referred to them directly with the use of an epithet: "the poor." It is a term he used only two times in his gospel — the first time being the above-mentioned encounter with the man with many possessions. Mark does not call him "young," by the way.

The only other time Mark used this epithet was when Jesus was anointed with an expensive oil by the woman at Bethany. Some of those present (Mark does not call them disciples) rebuked her, saying that the ointment could have been sold for a considerable amount of money, with the money going to "the poor" (Mark 14:5). If these objectors were Essenes, what they probably were saying was that the money could have been given to the "order." Jesus responded: "You always have the poor with you, and you can show kindness to them whenever you wish, but you will not always have me" (Mark 14:7). This would seem to be a callous statement if Jesus was actually talking about those living in real poverty — but if he was referring to a community which pooled its income and called themselves "the poor," the meaning would be much different.

Was Jesus an Essene?

Mark wrote nothing about Jesus' life before his baptism by John the Baptist. Did a young Jesus, like Josephus, ever study the various sects of Judaism, or spend time in the wilderness under the tutelage of an ascetic like Barus (John the Baptist, perhaps)? All we really know from Mark about Jesus' life before his public ministry is that he was a carpenter in Nazareth (Mark 6:3), but this neither confirms nor denies that he was an Essene, as we have seen that Essenes worked in professions like anyone else.

Furthermore, although there are many similarities between the customs of the Essenes as Josephus reported them and the ministry of Jesus as Mark described it, there were also a few differences. The primary difference centered on sabbath observance. For example, Josephus tells us that the Essenes "abstain from seventh-day work more rigidly than any other Jew." Jesus' disciples, on the other hand, gleaned grain on the sabbath (Mark 2:23) — something Essenes apparently would not do.

If Jesus had ever been an Essene, he probably had parted with them at some point over certain issues somewhere along the way — although it seems he may have continued to follow several of their practices and relied on their community for hospitality as he traveled.

Was Mark an Essene?

A related and perhaps equally intriguing question might be: "Was *Mark* an Essene?" Was this a "party" to which he belonged or had belonged at one time? The short answer to that must also be "we really don't know." Since he referred to virtually every other major group in Judaism at the time, but not the Essenes, our first response might be that he was not. However, since Mark never mentioned himself directly or by name in his narrative, it might also follow that he wouldn't mention the group to which he belonged by name, either.

Furthermore, Mark seems to have had a thorough understanding of the Essene way of life, and if a characteristic of being human is trying to remake our heroes in our own image, it is possible that Mark's writing of the gospel was colored by his point of view. He certainly related the story of Jesus' ministry in a way that suggests it was influenced by the Essenes.

Another clue, however, is found in the description of the "certain young man" who followed Jesus and the disciples into the garden after the Passover meal. Mark makes a point of saying that this young man was wearing a linen garment. This might seem like an insignificant detail, and we might even wonder why Mark would mention it. However, Josephus tells us that a linen garment is precisely what the Essenes would wear at a meal. This detail may be Mark's way of identifying himself as an Essene. If the house where Jesus and his disciples ate the Passover meal was an Essene building (more on this below), and if this young man had been present in that home during the meal, I can imagine him — impressed by the great teacher and miracle worker who had just left the house — slipping away and following to the garden, still wearing the garment he had worn at the meal.

Which brings us back to Holy Week to look for other clues about Mark.

Holy Week and the Importance of Bethany

Jesus' entrance into Jerusalem in chapter 11 marked the beginning of Holy Week, and it was from Bethany that Jesus comes:

> When they were approaching Jerusalem, at Bethphage and Bethany...
> — Mark 11:1

Other gospels tell us that Bethany was where Mary and Martha lived. John said that Lazarus was their brother. Both Luke and John report that Jesus visited their home before Holy Week.

Mark, however, mentioned neither Mary nor Martha nor Lazarus, nor does he report any previous visits of Jesus to Bethany. Even so, Bethany becomes the "home base" for Jesus during Holy Week. Was there an Essene community in Bethany? Josephus did tell us they were everywhere. Could Bethany have been Mark's home? Whatever it was, the town of Bethany and the people in and around it seem to have been familiar to Mark and significant to Jesus. If it was Mark's home, or the home of someone Mark knew well, it would have provided Mark with a front row seat to the events of Holy Week, and firsthand knowledge of Jesus' comings and goings during that time.

The Enigmatic Instructions

It was from Bethany that Jesus gave two of his disciples these enigmatic instructions:

> Go into the village ahead of you, and immediately as you enter it, you will find tied there a colt that has never been ridden; untie it and bring it. If anyone says to you, "Why are you doing this?" just say this, "The Lord needs it and will send it back here immediately."
> — Mark 11:2b-3

If we knew nothing of the Essenes, these instructions would seem somehow strange and mysterious, but when viewed in the context of the kind of hospitality and sharing of possessions that pervaded the Essene community — even toward strangers — these instructions make perfect sense.

Later that week, Jesus gave a set of similar instructions when he sent two of his disciples into Jerusalem to find a place to eat the Passover meal:

> Go into the city, and a man carrying a jar of water will meet you; follow him, and wherever he enters, say to the owner of the house, "The teacher asks, Where is my guest room where I may eat the Passover with my disciples?" He will show you a large room upstairs, furnished and ready.
> — Mark 14:13b-15a

Again, if we knew nothing of the Essenes we might wonder who this man was and how Jesus knew he would be there. However, if Jesus was taking advantage of the Essene network of homes and hospitality, the wonder disappears. Furthermore, a man carrying a jar of water — a job that might otherwise be consigned to a woman — would surely be an Essene, and the house to which he was taking the water would then be an Essene house. If the disciples asked at such a house for a place to observe the Passover, Jesus knew it would be provided.

The Anointing at Bethany and the Unnamed Woman

This episode occurred during Holy Week in the home of one Simon the Leper (Mark 14:3ff). "Leper" does not necessarily mean afflicted with what we today commonly call leprosy, as this word could refer to a number of conditions of the skin. Whatever the condition was, however, the appellation was enough to identify this Simon as distinct from other Simons mentioned in Mark's gospel, such as Simon Peter or Simon the brother of Jesus or Simon of Cyrene. It was while Jesus was in the house of this Simon the Leper that an unnamed woman anoints Jesus with nard.

Nard was a rare and expensive ointment. It was used as a perfume — as an ingredient in some kinds of incense, in herbal medicine, and in the anointing of the dead.

While it is not clear what the intention of the woman was in anointing Jesus, it is clear that some of those who witnessed the anointing did not like it, as we have already noted earlier in this chapter. Jesus, however, defended her and her action and gave it a meaning that perhaps even she had not intended:

> Let her alone; why do you trouble her? She has performed a good service for me... she has anointed my body before-hand for its burial.
> — Mark 14:6-8

Jesus then added some very touching and poignant words about this woman's action:

> Truly I tell you, wherever the good news is proclaimed in the whole world, what she has done will be told in remembrance of her.
> — Mark 14:9

But Mark never told us her name.

He told us the name of the owner of the house in which this happened. He told us the name of the man who carried Jesus' cross. He told us the name of the man who claimed Jesus' body and put it in a tomb.

But he didn't tell us the name of the woman who anointed his body for burial, an action he says will be remembered "as long as the gospel story is told."

Who was this woman?

When Matthew related this story, he copied Mark, telling it essentially as Mark had recorded it, also without mentioning who the woman might have been. Matthew probably didn't know who she was.

John's gospel told us that she was Mary, the sister of Lazarus. If that were so, we can understand the reason she might have poured such expensive perfume on Jesus — the gratitude she must have felt because Jesus had raised her brother from the grave!

Luke, on the other hand, omitted this story altogether. He mentioned neither this woman, nor Simon the Leper, nor any anointing of Jesus during Holy Week.

Luke did have another, somewhat similar story found in Luke 7:36-50, in which a woman anointed Jesus with "an alabaster flask of ointment." Jesus was also reclining at table in the home of a man named Simon, but that Simon, according to Luke, was a Pharisee (and definitely not an Essene).

It's not the first time that Luke had rewritten his gospel in ways that were different from Mark, especially when it came to women. Consider the story of the death of John the Baptist, for example. Mark told us that the daughter of Herodias, at her mother's urging, asked for the head of John the Baptist on a plate (John the Baptist had condemned the marriage of Herod and Herodias, as Herodias had been his brother's wife). Matthew repeated the story pretty much the same way Mark did. Luke, however, reported that Herod had cut off the head of the Baptist, but he omitted the references to the women altogether.

It's important to note that Luke was very sympathetic toward women. Whereas Matthew told the birth narrative from the point of view of Joseph, Luke focused upon Mary and Elizabeth. There was not a single woman in Luke's gospel portrayed in a negative light.

But Luke did not include the story of the anointing at Bethany. Why would he leave out a story about a woman whose action Jesus so highly commended?

Could the answer be political? Did Mark and Luke belong to different "parties"? If this home and this woman were special to Mark, did Luke leave out this story for the same reason he left out the "signature" passage of the *neaniskos* in the Garden of Gethsemane — to diminish or discredit the group of which Mark was a part? (We will return to this theme later.)

Mark, however, included it. Who was she?

One Mother's Day, during a sermon, I fancied that it was Mark's own mother. Whoever she was — mother, sister, friend, or otherwise — this person was special to Mark, but like Mark himself, remained unnamed.

"The Poor" and the Ebionites

Before we leave the question as to who Mark was and who may have influenced him, we must say a word about another group who called themselves "the poor": the Ebionites.

As the early church developed, various groups emerged that held differing beliefs about Jesus and about how a follower of Christ should live. Some of those differences are seen in the Acts of the Apostles, with the most obvious one, perhaps, being the aforementioned controversy about circumcision (Acts 15:1). Other issues included what kinds of food to eat (1 Corinthians 8:1-13), whether or not to marry (1 Corinthians 7:25-38), whether to consort with and "evangelize" Gentiles (Acts 10:1-48), and even how someone should wear their hair or cover their head (1 Corinthians 11:2-16).

As the church spread and grew, sects that were not considered mainstream were deemed heretical, and most

of their writings were destroyed. The only real information we have about such groups comes from what their
mainstream opponents wrote about them. Epiphanius
of Salamis, for example, writing about AD 350, described
eighty different heresies and dozens of sects.

One of the sects he mentioned was the Ebionites. The
name is derived from the Hebrew word which means "the
poor." Epiphanius says that the group originated about
the time of the fall of Jerusalem. He admitted that the
group had evolved over time, but among the beliefs he
listed are:

• They did not believe that Jesus was born of a virgin nor
conceived by the Holy Spirit
• They believed that Jesus was adopted as the Son of
God at his baptism, when the Spirit came upon him as
a dove
• They adhered to observance of the sabbath and circum-
cision
• They were vegetarians

Was Mark an Ebionite?
Mark certainly does not seem to be an Ebionite in the way
they are described by Epiphanius in AD 350. However,
he wrote at just the time Epiphanius says the Ebionites
formed, around the fall of Jerusalem. Furthermore, Mark
mentioned nothing of a virgin birth.

Most importantly, perhaps, was the story in Mark in
which we meet Jesus for the first time — his baptism. This
could be construed as an adoption story — especially in
the absence of birth narratives. In this opening scene of
the gospel, Mark reported that the spirit descended upon
Jesus as a dove and he heard the words: "You are my beloved son" (Mark 1:11). These words were a quote from
Psalm 2, which is often called a "royal psalm." It would be

read at the coronation of a king, and it calls the king the Lord's "anointed" (the Hebrew word is *mashiah*, which can also be translated as "messiah"). The words "you are my son" are also spoken, as if by God, to the new king, followed by the words "today I have begotten you." By placing this story first and omitting a story about the birth, Mark may have been articulating the Ebionite doctrine that Jesus was not *born* the "Son of God" but was instead *adopted* the day of his baptism.

Who Was Mark? To What "Party" Did He Belong?
From our study so far, it is intriguing to suggest that Mark was

- an Essene who lived in or near Jerusalem,
- the son of a woman named Mary,
- related to the woman who anointed Jesus at Bethany,
- the young man present in the garden when Jesus was arrested,
- at the tomb on Easter morning,
- a companion to Paul and Barnabas,
- a cousin to Barnabas, or
- an early Ebionite who did not believe in the virgin birth.

The truth is, he may have been none of these, all of them, or somewhere in the middle. We don't know for sure — but Mark has more to tell.

---

1. *Bellum Judaeorum* translated by G.A. Williamson (New York: Penguin Books, 1970).

Chapter 9

When Did Mark Write?

If Mark wrote to address issues facing the church of his day, discerning *when* he wrote might help us better understand what compelled him to write.

The Latest Date Possible
The oldest fragments of extant manuscripts with quotations from the gospel of Mark date from the early third century (around AD 200), but it is believed that Mark's gospel was written well before this date for several reasons. For one thing, Justin Martyr, who died in AD 165, referred in one of his letters to what may have been the gospel of Mark. More definitively, however, we also know that a heretic named Marcion, who died in AD 160, used an edited version of Luke's gospel as a source for authority. Since Luke used Mark as a resource to write his gospel, Mark had to be written sometime before that — no later than AD 140 or 150 to be sure.

The Earliest Date Possible
The *earliest* that Mark could have been written, of course, was immediately after the crucifixion. Mark told us that Jesus was crucified when Pontius Pilate was the procurator of Judea. Pilate ruled from AD 26 to 36, so Mark could not have been written before the beginning of his governorship. Mark also mentioned by name Herod (Antipas), who ruled Galilee, and Herod's brother Philip, who ruled the region north of Galilee, but their reigns overlapped that of Pilate, so this information does not help us narrow down the earliest date any further.

However, if Mark was writing to address specific concerns that were arising within the early church, it probably took a number of years for those concerns to congeal to the point where a written gospel was needed to do so. Since Paul's letters are generally dated no earlier than AD 50, we might assume that Mark did not write before then, either.

This gives us a range of about 100 years, from about AD 50 to AD 150, as to when the gospel could have been written.

Is there anything else in the gospel itself that might help us narrow down when Mark wrote?

A clue may be found in chapter 13.

The Destruction of Jerusalem
The chapter begins with Jesus and the disciples in Jerusalem during Holy Week. They are standing outside the temple when one of the disciples — sounding like a gawking tourist on his first visit to the big city, or perhaps more appropriately like a student on his first field trip — said to Jesus:

> Look, Teacher, what large stones and what large buildings!
> — Mark 13:1

Jesus responds with these words:

> Do you see these great buildings? Not one stone will be left here upon another; all will be thrown down.
> — Mark 13:2

Some people think that Jesus was speaking about the fact that nothing built by human hands lasts forever. "Time and tide" will destroy all things, sooner or later.

However, the words used here by Jesus betray a different meaning. The word translated as "will be thrown down" is the Greek word *kataluthe*. This word does not refer to an eroding away or even a falling down. It means, rather, to physically take something down in a destructive way. For example, this same word is used in 14:58 when someone accuses Jesus of saying that he will "destroy" the temple, and then rebuild it again in three days. There is no reason to render this word any differently when Jesus uses it here: "all of these buildings will be *destroyed*."

Mark reported that Peter, Andrew, James, and John certainly thought that this was what Jesus meant. After all, if Jesus was just talking about natural erosion over time, they wouldn't have to ask the question "when?" However, that's exactly what they ask in the very next verse: "When will this be, and what will be the sign that all these things are about to be accomplished?" (Mark 13:4).

Jesus answered in a discourse that is often called "the little apocalypse."

The Little Apocalypse (Mark 13)

Apocalyptic literature is a complex and mysterious genre which was especially popular in the years 200 BC to AD 100. It often used cataclysmic events and conflicts, sometimes cosmic in scope, along with end-time imagery, in order to deal with issues pertaining to the age in which the authors lived. In other words, the authors of apocalyptic literature weren't talking about the future — they were talking about themselves. The revelation of John and the book of Daniel are two biblical books that are apocalyptic in nature.

Chapter 13 of Mark is often called "the little apocalypse" because it draws upon words and images from Daniel and other sources as Jesus spoke of a cataclysm and an end yet to come. It is a remarkable discourse — the longest uninterrupted speech of Jesus in the gospel of Mark — culminating in the triumphant return of Jesus as an apocalyptic "Son of Man," and concluding with a word addressing his delay in coming. Of course, as Jesus talked about wars, famines, earthquakes, and unspeakable horror, he could be describing almost any era from the beginning of time to the present day. However, if apocalyptic literature used such imagery to speak to the age in which it was written, then we must ask ourselves what in this chapter might give us clues as to the specific time when Mark wrote. There are several passages that give us help.

The Desolating Sacrilege...
In Mark 13:4, Mark recorded Jesus as saying:

> But when you see the desolating sacrilege set up where it ought not to be (let the reader understand), then those in Judea must flee to the mountains...
> — Mark 13:14

The disciples had asked for a sign, and Jesus gave it to them in the form of a "desolating sacrilege." This term is a quote from Daniel, who several times referred to "an abomination that desolates":

> Forces sent by him shall occupy and profane the temple and fortress. They shall abolish the regular burnt offering and set up the abomination that makes desolate.
> — Daniel 11:31; cf also Daniel 9:27 and 12:11

Daniel was writing about the time period before the Maccabean revolt, when Hellenizers abolished the temple offering and set up an altar to Zeus in the temple. This led in part to the subsequent revolt. Mark saw a parallel in what was happening in his own age with what was written in Daniel. This is why he used the phrase "let the reader understand" immediately after his reference to the desolating sacrilege. He wanted the reader to understand the parallel he was drawing.

Unfortunately, it is not perfectly clear as to what the "desolating sacrilege" is of which Jesus spoke. Despite Mark's warning of "let the reader understand," we do not totally understand.

Help, however, is given to us by Luke, in the way he changed what Mark had written. Luke apparently felt people (like us) would not understand what was being said, so when Luke wrote his gospel, he tried to clarify what Mark records by eliminating portions of Mark's text, including the words "desolating sacrilege" and "let the reader understand." He replaced them with these words:

> When you see Jerusalem surrounded by armies, then know that its desolation has come near. Then those in Judea must flee...
> — Luke 21:20-21

Luke believed that Mark was referring to a time of war when armies would besiege and destroy Jerusalem, and that people must flee Jerusalem before it happened. This is a conclusion to which we could have come without Luke's aid, but his interpretation of Mark helps confirm this for us.

Two events between the years AD 50 and AD 150 seem to fit this situation:

1) the revolt of AD 66-70 and
2) the Bar Kochba Revolt of AD 132

The Revolt of AD 66-70
This revolt and the circumstances leading up to it were chronicled by Josephus, the Jewish general who at first

participated in the revolt. Leading a force in Galilee against the Romans, his army was defeated and he was captured. According to his account in *Bellum Judaeorum*, he was almost killed by his captors, eventually was befriended by them, and ultimately even tried — unsuccessfully — to persuade the Jews in Jerusalem to surrender in order to avoid further bloodshed and prevent the destruction of the city. In his book he also detailed the revolutionary fervor that gripped the region in the years preceding the revolt, and told of several people who made messianic claims and led various other attempts against Rome prior to AD 66.

The revolt of AD 66 itself began, according to Josephus, in the coastal city of Caesarea. Religious tensions between Jews and Greeks provided the spark, with anti-tax sentiment also playing a part. The revolt spread quickly throughout Israel, and at first the Jewish rebels were successful against the Romans. However, Rome eventually crushed all opposition, beginning with the coastline and then moving through Galilee before turning to Judea. Jerusalem itself fell in AD 70, and the temple was destroyed in the process.

The destruction of life and property during the conflict as described by Josephus was horrific. The Romans were relentless and sometimes ruthless in their attacks on the Jewish insurgents. The insurgents themselves were also ruthless — and not just against the Roman enemy but also amongst themselves. During the siege of Jerusalem, for example, anyone advocating surrender was killed by the rebels. Mark may have had this situation in mind when he quoted Jesus as saying:

> Brother will betray brother to death, and a father his child, and children will rise against parents and have them put to death.
> — Mark 13:12

Meanwhile, those trying to escape Jerusalem who were captured by the Romans were crucified on a hill facing Jerusalem, with as many as 500 a day being killed. Between executions, disease, and battle deaths, Josephus reported that over 1.1 million people died and nearly 100,000 were enslaved. While these numbers may seem to be exaggerations (Josephus, after all, was writing as a ward of Rome, and some of what he wrote has to be considered from that perspective), they give a sense of the magnitude of the conflict and the hopelessness felt by those living during this time. Mark summed up the hopelessness, in the words of Jesus, this way:

> Woe to those who are pregnant and to those who are nursing infants in those days! Pray that it may not be in winter. For in those days there will be suffering, such as has not been from the beginning of the creation that God created until now, no, and never will be.
> — Mark 13:17-19

The Bar Kochba Revolt of AD 132

The other cataclysm to which Mark may have been referring in this chapter is the Bar Kochba Revolt of AD 132. Roman historian Cassio Dio reported that 500,000 were killed, the city of Jerusalem was destroyed, and another fifty fortified cities and 985 villages were razed. The devastation resulting from this revolt may have been even worse than the war of AD 66-70, and some historians mark this date as the beginning of the Jewish Diaspora. AD 132 may seem late for the writing of the gospel, but it does fall within our preliminary parameters of the latest the gospel could have been written — although it would eliminate the author as the eyewitness in the garden or at the empty tomb.

There is, however, a passage in Mark which argues against such a late date.

"This Generation Will Not Pass Away..."

The most compelling argument against a late date is that Mark reported Jesus as saying that these things would happen within the generation that was alive during Jesus' own lifetime:

> Truly I tell you, this generation will not pass away until all these things have taken place.
> — Mark 13:30

By the year AD 132, no one who was living at the time of the crucifixion of Jesus was still around. If Mark was writing from after AD 132, we would think he would not quote Jesus saying "all these things" would happen before his generation had ended. This suggests that the destruction of which Mark wrote is not from the revolt of AD 132 but rather the revolt of AD 66-70. If this is correct, AD 70, becomes the earliest the gospel could have been written.

Why Not *Before* the Temple Destruction?

Is it possible that Mark wrote before the destruction of the temple? After all, if Jesus was predicting the future, then Mark could have written before the revolution itself!

However, if Jesus really was predicting the future, he wasn't a very good fortuneteller. For example, he told his disciples, in verse 24:

> ...in those days, after that suffering... then they will see "the Son of Man coming in clouds"...

However, "in those days," after the destruction of the temple in AD 70 (and even after the Bar Kochba Revolt of AD 132), the Son of Man did *not* appear. If the delay was going to be as long as at least 2,000 years (our present day), why tell us only of the soon-to-occur wars in which the temple and/or Jerusalem would be destroyed? Why stop there? Why not tell us what other things would happen — and that it might be a *very* long time before the Son of Man would return. Why tell us "all these things will happen before this generation passes away"?

The most obvious answer is that Jesus stopped there because that was the time period in which Mark wrote. He was not concerned with future generations; he was writing to those in his own time. If Mark was using apocalyptic imagery to address the age in which he lived, this places the writing of his gospel within the generation following the crucifixion, but no earlier than the destruction of the temple in AD 70.

The Latest Date, Revisited

We can now revisit the question as to the latest date Mark's gospel could have been written. If it was written within the generation of those who were alive at the time of Jesus' crucifixion, when would that generation end?

If the biblical "three score and ten" (70 years) is used as a measure, the generation that was alive at Jesus' crucifixion around AD 30 would end around AD 100. However, if Jesus was addressing adults who were standing before him and not talking about those just being born, we might shave a few years away from that. AD 85 might be considered to be a good end date for the generation following the resurrection of Jesus.

We can conjecture, therefore, that Mark was written within a fifteen-year window between AD 70 and AD 85 — and probably closer to the beginning of that window than the end. This would put the date the composition of Mark at about the same time Josephus was writing — around AD 72.

This date would also fit our time frame for the *ne-aniskos* in the garden to be the author of the gospel, for that Greek word refers to someone between the ages of 15 and 40. If Mark was as young as 15 at the time of the crucifixion (and there is a certain romance to imagining a young person of 15 stealthily following Jesus and the disciples into the garden after having been with him during the Passover meal), he would have been about 55 years old in AD 70. On the other hand, if he was as old as 40 at the time of the crucifixion, in AD 70 he would have been 80 or so — by no means too old to write a book!

From Whence Does Mark Write?

If Mark wrote just after the war and the devastation that swept through Jerusalem, it would seem unlikely that he wrote from that city. Indeed, in the "little apocalypse" he warned those in Judea to leave and "flee to the hills" in order to avoid the suffering that would accompany the revolt, and it is possible that he himself was writing from one of those hills. Specific locations might include the hills of Galilee. After all, Mark reported that Jesus told the disciples he was going to Galilee after the resurrection (and the young man told the women the same thing). However, Josephus told us that the cities of Galilee did not escape the war and provided no refuge from the wrath of the Romans. Mark, writing just after the war, would have known this and would surely not have Jesus tell people to go there to avoid the conflagration. Furthermore, I have already posited that Mark was not talking about the geographic region of Galilee when he used this word.

Other hills to which people fled included the summit fortress of Masada, but it is unlikely that Mark wrote from that location.

However, the hills of Nabatea are a possibility. Nabatea was across the Dead Sea from Masada, and its hills were higher than Masada. Mark may have shown an affinity for that region in his account of the death of John the Baptist, when he reported that John was killed because he had condemned Herod for marrying his brother Philip's wife. What Mark did not report, but what he surely knew, was that in marrying Philip's wife, Herod had divorced his own wife, who happened to be the daughter of the king of Nabatea. By condemning Herod for this action, Mark may have gained the favor of the Nabateans, who did not participate in the revolt against Rome and could have afforded safety for those fleeing Rome's wrath, and become a haven for Mark to compose his gospel.

Another location that has been suggested, because of certain Latinisms in the text, is the city of Rome. Latinisms, however, would not be peculiar to Rome.

On the other hand, if Mark was the same person as John Mark of Acts, the last time we know of his location — perhaps around AD 55 — is when he and Barnabas are heading for Cypress, which, according to Luke, was Barnabas' native land. If Mark was a cousin to Barnabas, Mark likely had family in Cypress, as well, which could have provided him support. Furthermore, the Jewish community in Cypress was able to avoid the persecutions that occurred in Israel and Rome during the Revolt of AD 66-70, and the relative safety of Cypress may have afforded Mark the setting and stability he needed to write. It was not until the Bar Kochba Revolt in the second century that Cypress experienced the kind of problems that were occurring in Israel.

The truth is that the gospel could have been written in almost any location — from Nabatea to Rome to anywhere in between or beyond. What is more important is what he wrote and why — a question to which we shall now turn.

Chapter 10

Heroes and Villains:
Why Did Mark Write?

The gospel of John was written, its author tells us, "so that you may come to believe that Jesus is the Messiah, the Son of God, and that through believing you may have life in his name" (John 20:31).

Luke told us that he wrote because he wanted to write an "orderly account" (Luke 1:3). The Greek which is usually rendered as "an orderly account" can also be rendered "more accurately," which suggests that Luke apparently felt that those who had already written (including Mark) hadn't told the real story.

Mark, on the other hand, did not explicitly give a reason for writing his book, but if he wrote in order to address issues that were facing the church at the time of his writing, what were some of the issues facing the church in AD 72 which we might expect him to address?

One issue already mentioned is the delay of the return of Jesus as the triumphant Son of Man, and we will turn to this first. A second issue has also been touched upon: the persecution of the church at the hands of the Romans and others. A third issue, not often mentioned but just as real, was the generation which had led the community in its infancy was being killed or dying off, and the question arose as to who would take up the reins.

The methodology I will follow in exploring the reasons as to why Mark wrote is one you might expect of an English literature major when examining any work of literature — by looking at how the author portrayed the various characters in his or her narrative. Who were the heroes? Who were the villains? Who was presented as a sympathetic character? Who was unsympathetic? Who did Jesus commend? Who did he condemn? Who got a mixed reception?

Finally, in examining these issues we also need to ask this question: "Which of the reasons for writing best explains why Mark did not place resurrection appearances after the story of the empty tomb?"

A. The Delay of the Coming Son of Man

The main protagonist — the hero of the story, if you will — was Jesus himself, seen most heroically, perhaps, in the figure Mark called the Son of Man, whom Mark expected to return triumphantly, but whose arrival has not yet occurred. Does the lack of resurrection appearances at the end of the gospel have anything to do with the delay of the appearance of Jesus as the Son of Man? Before we answer that question, let's take a look at this "Son of Man" term, which is used fourteen times in the gospel of Mark. It would be very familiar to Mark's original readers, with varied meaning.

Son of Man as "Human Being"
On the one hand, the term "son of man" is sometimes used idiomatically to refer to an ordinary human being. This is seen, for example, in the poetry of Psalm 8:

> ...what is man, that you think of him? The son of man that you care for him?
> — Psalm 8:4 (RSV)

It is important to note a feature of Hebrew poetry at work here: the principle of "parallelism." Among other things, Hebrew poets and prophets usually wrote their poetry in a series of couplets, with the first part of the verse conveying a single thought or idea, and the second parallel part saying it again — using different words to express the same thing. (In English, poets often rhyme words at the ends of phrases; Hebrew poets might be said to rhyme the phrases themselves — although they sometimes varied the pace by using contrasting or complementing phrases.) Applying this principle to the verse in Psalm 8 suggests that the word "man" in the first half of the couplet and the words "son of man" in the second half are "saying the same thing twice." In this case they both mean human beings in general.

This may be the way this term is used at times in Mark's gospel, particularly in the poetic couplet about the sabbath:

> The sabbath was made for man, not man for the sabbath; so
> the son of man is lord even of the sabbath.
> — Mark 2:27 (RSV)

"Human beings" may also be the meaning Jesus had in mind the second time this term appears, when he announced "the son of man has authority on earth to forgive sins" (Mark 2:10). Whether those who first heard these words understood it this way is hard to say. Mark is delightfully ambiguous on this point.

Son of Man as "Messianic" Figure
People who heard Jesus use this term would also have heard another meaning, for the words "son of man" had come to have messianic implications. Consider these words from the book of Daniel:

> I saw in the night visions, and behold,
> with the clouds of heaven

89

there came one like a son of man,
and he came to the Ancient of Days
and was presented before him.

And to him was given dominion
and glory and kingdom,
that all peoples, nations, and languages
should serve him;
his dominion is an everlasting dominion,
which shall not pass away,
and his kingdom one
that shall not be destroyed.
— Daniel 7:13-14 (RSV)

Whatever Daniel may have meant when he wrote this passage and used the term "son of man," it came to represent a figure whom God would send to rescue God's people — a messiah — and in Mark, Jesus used this term several times, with seeming messianic implications.

This seems clear the third time Jesus used this term in Mark. The context was Peter's confession of Jesus as the Messiah (Mark 8:29). Jesus then told them, for the first time, the nature of his messiahship:

Then he began to teach them that the Son of Man must undergo great suffering, and be rejected by the elders, the chief priests, and the scribes, and be killed, and after three days rise again.
— Mark 8:31

When Peter heard these words, he immediately took Jesus aside and "rebuked" him. Jesus in turn rebuked Peter and in the very next paragraph said to the crowd:

Those who are ashamed of me and of my words in this adulterous and sinful generation, of them the Son of Man will also be ashamed when he comes in the glory of his Father with the holy angels.
— Mark 8:38

The juxtaposition of these verses makes it clear that Mark believed Jesus to be the Son of Man who would suffer, die, rise again, and then triumphantly return. Jesus then added:

> Truly I tell you, there are some standing here who will not taste death until they see that the kingdom of God has come with power.
> — Mark 9:1

Since this verse comes immediately after Jesus talked about the return of the Son of Man, we might assume that the "kingdom of God [coming] with power" and the arrival of the Son of Man are synonymous, but this is not perfectly clear. Certainly, the phrase "kingdom of God... come with power" is ambiguous enough to be open to interpretation, and Mark may not have been talking about the coming of the Son of Man but rather something else — perhaps the start of the church — and this certainly is a possibility. Since the Son of Man did not appear within Mark's lifetime, subsequent generations have been forced into such an interpretation. However, the next time the coming of the Son of Man is mentioned, the words are not so ambiguous:

> ...they will see "the Son of Man coming in clouds" with great power and glory. Then he will send out the angels, and gather his elect from the four winds, from the ends of the earth to the ends of heaven.
> From the fig tree learn its lesson: as soon as its branch becomes tender and puts forth its leaves, you know that summer is near. So also, when you see these things taking place, you know that he is near, at the very gates. Truly I tell you, this generation will not pass away until all these things have taken place. Heaven and earth will pass away, but my words will not pass away.
> — Mark 13:26-31

If "all these things" included the return of the Son of Man, it seems probable that Mark expected that return to occur during his lifetime — and we cannot fault Mark for this expectation. Paul taught this, as well (see, for example, 1 Thessalonians 4:15: "for we who are alive, who are left until the coming of the Lord... "). In fact, in every generation there have been those who believed that Jesus' return was imminent. As for Mark, we can imagine that he was so gripped by the message and ministry of Jesus that his expectation of a quick return was a natural outgrowth of his enthusiasm — and we can understand that those who shared this expectation and enthusiasm were asking the question of the disciples in chapter 13:4: "When will this be...?" At this point, however, Mark hedges his bets, saying that he can't answer that question because Jesus himself didn't know — only that it would be soon, adding a warning that they need to "keep alert":

> But about that day or hour no one knows, neither the angels in heaven, nor the Son, but only the Father. Beware, keep alert, for you do not know when the time will come.
> — Mark 13:32-33

To emphasize this point, Mark inserts a story about a master who goes on a journey, but whose return is delayed. He ends the parable with these words:

> Keep awake, for you do not know when the master of the house will come — in the **evening**, or at **midnight**, or at **cock-crow**, or at **dawn** — or else he may find you asleep when he comes suddenly.
> — Mark 13:35-36 (emphasis mine)

The Delayed Master: A Prelude to Gethsemane?
We soon discover that Mark — artisan that he was — had placed this story here not only as a commentary about

the coming of the Son of Man at some future date, but as a foretaste of what would happen later that very week, after Jesus arrived with the disciples in the Garden of Gethsemane. He took Peter, James, and John alone with him further into in the garden, and there he repeated the words of warning he had told them earlier that week: "keep awake." Jesus then went off to pray. When he came back (in the *evening*) he found them asleep; later he found them sleeping again at *midnight*. By *cockcrow* Peter had denied Jesus three times before, and at *dawn* when Jesus was handed over to Pilate, none of them were to be found!

No Resurrection Appearances?

Does Mark's omission of resurrection appearances have anything to do with the delayed return of the Son of Man? If so, it may be that he omitted such appearances because he believed that the risen Christ would not appear until he returned at the "end" as the Son of Man — whether that end would be in the near future or at some far away date.

Against this, however, stands the fact that if Mark was writing to address the delay of the return of Christ and to assure his followers that the Son of Man would be coming soon, his omission of resurrection appearances would add nothing to those assurances and might even be seen as undermining them.

Most importantly, Jesus told the disciples after the Last Supper that when he rises he will go before them to Galilee — a message which is repeated by the young man at the empty tomb when he told the women that they were to go to Galilee to see the risen Christ — but when Jesus spoke about the return of the Son of Man in the discourse called the little apocalypse, there was *no mention of Galilee!* Instead, the Son of Man would "gather his elect from the four winds" (Mark 13:27). Since it is not neces-sary to go to Galilee to wait for the arrival of a Son of Man, this suggests that seeing the resurrected Christ after the story of the empty tomb is unrelated to the return of the Son of Man. This means we need to look at other issues Mark's community was facing to discern his reason for choosing not to report resurrection appearances after the story of the empty tomb.

B. An *Apologia*

The Protagonists
If Jesus was the main protagonist in the story Mark wrote, he was not the only one. Beyond Jesus, there were several characters or groups whom Mark portrayed in a positive light. If not protagonists they were at least sympathetic characters of the gospel. They include, among others:

- John the Baptist
- Children (the ones to whom the kingdom of God be-longs)
- Women, including the woman who anointed Jesus and those who had followed him from Galilee and watched the crucifixion
- Sinners such as tax collectors and others who did not live according to the rituals and traditions prescribed by the Pharisees
- Those who were sick, disabled, or otherwise unclean
- The crowd for whom Jesus had compassion
- Joseph of Arimathea
- The young man at the tomb
- The anonymous person who cast out demons
- The poor

The Antagonists

The antagonists, on the other hand, were those unsympathetic characters whom Mark portrayed in a negative light:

- Pharisees
- Herodians
- Scribes
- Chief Priests and Sadducees (the chief priests would have come from the Sadducean group)
- Elders (members of the Sanhedrin)
- Jesus' hometown neighbors
- Judas
- The money changers

Excepting Judas and Jesus' hometown neighbors, the majority of the antagonists listed above might have been considered a part of the religious establishment — the "leadership" of the religious and temporal life of the Jews — starting with the Pharisees. Josephus told us that the Pharisees were "the most authoritative exponents of the law" and called them "the leading sect." In some ways there was much for which to commend them. They believed, for example, in a just God who rewarded those who lived good lives and who punished those who did not. They believed in an afterlife and that every soul was imperishable. They also believed it a duty to care for the aged.

Even so, Mark made it clear that there was no love lost between Jesus and the Pharisees. For his part, Jesus saw the main sin of the Pharisees as being hypocrisy (Mark 7:6), and he missed no opportunity to denounce them for it (see especially Mark 7:9-13 where Jesus seems to condemn the Pharisees for putting monetary support of the Pharisees ahead of caring for the elderly). As for the Pharisees, they were among the first to oppose Jesus. Among other things, they were upset that he ate with "sinners and tax collectors" (Mark 2:6). They also complained when Jesus' disciples gleaned grain from a field on the sabbath, saying that they were doing what was not lawful on the sabbath. Finally, they decided that Jesus needed to be eliminated after he healed a man on the sabbath: "The Pharisees went out and immediately conspired with the Herodians against him, how to destroy him" (Mark 3:6).

The Greek word rendered by the editors of the NRSV as "destroy" (*apollumi*) can variously be translated as "destroy," "ruin," or "kill," so it is unclear if at this point the intent of the Pharisees and Herodians is to kill Jesus or merely discredit him. Whatever their intent, what began as a conspiracy among the Herodians and Pharisees was later enjoined by the scribes and chief priests when Jesus arrived in Jerusalem and overturned the tables of the money changers in the temple. At that point they, too, looked for a way to *apollumi* Jesus (Mark 11:18). Ultimately they did this by turning him over to the Roman authorities as a "pretender to the throne" and revolutionary activist. Mark told us, however, that they were afraid to arrest him in public because the crowds supported Jesus (Mark 12:12). They got their opportunity when Judas Iscariot agreed to deliver Jesus to them (Mark 14:10-12).

Jesus Accused of Insurrection and Terrorism
When Jesus was arrested — away from the crowds — in Gethsemene, he said: "Have you come out with swords and clubs to arrest me — as though I were a *lestes*?" This word is usually translated in the New Testament as "thief" or "bandit" — Jesus called the temple a den of *lestes* in Mark 11:17 — but that word can also be translated as "freedom-fighter," "revolutionary," or even "terrorist," depending on the context and one's point of view.

Josephus, for example, usually used the word that way when he wrote his account of the Jewish war against Rome. Those opposing Rome were not thieves but revolutionaries and terrorists. In the context of Jesus' arrest, "revolutionary" or "terrorist" would seem an appropriate rendering instead of "thief," as well. Jesus, after all, was nowhere accused of being a thief. He was accused, however, of being "king of the Jews," out to overthrow Rome.

Since one of those with Jesus in Gethsemane (Mark doesn't tell us who) drew a sword and cut off the ear of the high priest's servant, some have suggested that Jesus' disciples were armed for the purpose of fighting Rome. Carrying a weapon, however, was not necessarily an indication of revolutionary intent. All Essenes, for example, carried weapons to defend themselves against *lestes* while traveling, and some of those following Jesus may have done the same. There was certainly no indication anywhere in Mark's gospel or any other source that Jesus or his followers intended to conduct armed revolutionary activity.

This accusation of being a revolutionary, however, was pressed during Jesus' interrogation. One of the charges leveled against him was that he had said he would "destroy the temple":

> Some stood up and gave false testimony against him, saying "We heard him say, 'I will destroy this temple that is made with hands, and in three days I will build another, not made with hands.'"
> — Mark 14:57-58

If Jesus spoke words to this effect (Mark called the testimony false, although John affirmed that Jesus did in fact say this), we might interpret this today to mean that Jesus was talking about the end of the power of the law and the beginning of a new community we now call the church. Those who first heard it, however, may have understood it as a threat against the ruling establishment. Even so, Jesus remained silent in the face of this and every accusation. He finally gave his opponents the ammunition they needed when the high priest asked him point blank: "Are you the messiah, the Son of the blessed one?" and Jesus responded: "I am." Jesus then went on to quote verses from Daniel and the Psalms:

> ...and "you will see the Son of Man seated at the right hand of the Power," and "coming with the clouds of heaven."
> — Mark 14:62

The high priest interpreted Jesus' response as "blasphemy," which in and of itself was not a reason to hand Jesus over to Pilate, but as these words could also be interpreted as an intent to start a revolution, the high priest was able to turn Jesus over to Pilate as a messianic rebel.

This brings us to the Romans — a group I did not classify as either protagonist or antagonist in the list at the beginning of this section.

The Romans

The Romans certainly were not protagonists of Mark's gospel. Few people in the Middle East deemed them heroes, and no one expected Jesus to commend them, or for Mark to treat them sympathetically.

And yet, Mark did not portray the Romans as a part of the conspiracy to kill Jesus. Throughout the gospel, whenever Jesus talked about his impending death, he never blamed — or even mentioned — Rome. In fact, until Holy Week itself there is no mention anywhere in Mark of Caesar, the governor, a centurion, or anyone else related to Rome. Even during Holy Week, Mark portrayed Jesus as no enemy of Rome.

This is demonstrated by the question the Pharisees and Herodians posed regarding taxes, "Is it lawful to pay taxes to the emperor, or not?" (Mark 12:14). Mark's contemporaries knew the incendiary nature of the question. Anti-tax sentiment and nationalist aspirations were intertwined and had a long history. Josephus reported that one of the first assignments of Herod, in 46 BC, was against *lestes* in Galilee — "freedom-fighters" who had supported Aristobulous, the last independent high priest and king, whom the Romans had overthrown in 63 BC. Herod had been able to suppress such rebellious activity, but his death in 3 BC opened the door to renewed unrest directed against Rome. In response, Judea was made a province in AD 6, ruled directly by a Roman governor instead of a Jewish king (although Herod, who practiced Judaism, was technically an Idumaean by birth whom many observant Jews of his day did not consider to be a Jew). Ironically, increased Roman oversight in turn led to more resistance. A census held immediately after the annexation as a province (census taking was for taxation purposes) also played a part in the unrest. Judah of Galilee, mentioned by both Josephus and Luke (in Acts 5:37), was one of those who led revolts during this time. Some may have hoped that Jesus would be just such a "revolutionary leader" who would oppose Roman rule, and the question about taxation would have been a litmus test for such a leader.

Jesus' answer, "Give to the emperor the things that are the emperor's, and to God the things that are God's" (Mark 12:17), reveals that Mark considered Jesus not to be a revolutionary in any political or military sense. According to Mark, Jesus accepted Roman rule and authority. As for the Romans, when Jesus was brought before Pilate, Pilate was portrayed as realizing that Jesus was not guilty of revolutionary activity but that "jealousy" had caused the religious authorities to want to eliminate Jesus (Mark 15:10).

Finally, and perhaps most significantly, it was a Roman who is the only person in the gospel who sincerely calls Jesus "God's Son":

> Now when the centurion, who stood facing him, saw that in this way he breathed his last, he said "Truly this man was God's Son!"
> — Mark 15:39

A Christian *Apologia*

The Greek word *apologia* does not mean "apology" in the common way we think if it today. Rather, an *apologia* is a defense or explanation. When applied to Christianity, it is understood as a defense or explanation of the faith, especially in the hopes of convincing one's audience to accept the faith — or at least to stop seeing it as a danger. The word is used many times in the New Testament, usually when someone is presenting a defense of the faith. Paul used this term, for example, when he made his *apologia* before King Agrippa (Acts 26:1ff) before he was sent to Rome for his appeal to Caesar.

If Mark's audience included the Gentile world in general and the Romans in particular, one of his reasons for writing may have been as an *apologia* — or defense — with the purpose of distancing Jesus and those who followed him from the religious establishment and others who led and supported the revolt against Rome. Mark wanted to make it clear that Jesus was not antagonistic toward Romans, and that those who made war against Rome — the leaders in Jerusalem and their allies — were no friends of Jesus, nor he of them.

No Resurrection Appearances?

If Mark omitted resurrection appearances in support of a Christian *apologia*, it may be that he did so because he felt that skeptical, even hostile, Romans and other Gentiles would be more tolerant and accepting of a religion whose messiah did not appear to others after his death.

Against this, of course, is the fact that the Romans themselves had traditions of heroes who ascended to the heavens, who became "gods," and who appeared to mortals on earth. Christians did not have to defend their faith by omitting appearances of a resurrected hero! Furthermore, Mark plainly stated that Jesus had overcome death and had risen. Omitting appearances would do nothing to change this affirmation — and might even undermine it. As such, this also seems to be an inadequate reason for omitting such appearances after the story of the empty tomb.

C. A Leadership Crisis in the Early Church

There were two other groups I passed over in the listing of protagonists and antagonists in the previous section:

• the family of Jesus, including Mary and Joseph
• the disciples

Looking through our "harmonized" glasses, *we* want to see these people as protagonists, as sympathetic characters, as important to the ministry of Jesus and the life of the early church.

But is that how Mark portrayed them? Let's turn first to Jesus' family.

The Family of Jesus

On the one hand, Mark had little to say about Jesus' family, which is telling enough. They appear but two times in the gospel. On the other hand, when they did appear they were not portrayed in a favorable light.

Jesus "Out of His Mind" (Mark 3:20-35)

The first time we meet the family is in the episode in which Jesus is said to be "out of his mind" (Mark 3:21). At first blush it may seem that Jesus' family is coming to his rescue, but close examination suggests that is not what Mark is saying.

The NRSV translates what Mark wrote regarding the first appearance of Jesus' family in this way:

> Then he went home; and the crowd came together again, so that they could not even eat. When his family heard it, they went out to restrain him, for people were saying, "He has gone out of his mind."
> — Mark 3:19b-21

It's important to note that the home spoken of here was in Capernaum, not Nazareth, as Jesus did not live with his biological family. Nevertheless, when his family heard of the crowds and the problems they caused, they appear to "restrain" Jesus. Mark, craftsman that he was, chose his words carefully, and the Greek word he chose when describing the restraining action of Jesus' family is *krateo*. Later in the gospel this same word is translated as "arrest" (Mark 12:12). Of course, in the case of Jesus' family, they may not have come to arrest Jesus, but neither were they coming to his rescue. We might say that they came to put him into protective custody; not to protect him from the actions of others but to protect him from himself, in the same way someone who is deemed insane might be committed to an institution. In fact, in the way

Mark crafted this encounter it seems that it actually may have been Jesus' family who considered him to be out of his mind, for a literal rendering of verse 21 would be:

> And those close to him (family/friends) went out to restrain him, for they said he was out of his mind.

Notice that the original Greek doesn't say that Jesus' family went to him because *people* said that Jesus was crazy (which is the way the NRSV has rendered this passage). Rather, it says "his family went out to restrain him, for *they* said he was out of his mind." Although Mark didn't precisely say who the "they" in this passage were, it doesn't appear to be the crowds who were coming to Jesus to be healed. Rather, a normal grammatical reading of this passage would suggest that "they" were Jesus' own family. The editors of the NRSV apparently didn't want to indicate that this might be Mark's intent, so they interpreted Mark's words and inserted the word "people" where it was not. However, Luke and Matthew didn't interpret it this way. They apparently thought Mark had Jesus' family in mind, for when they came to this episode, they both omitted this verse altogether.

If this was the only part of this episode that suggested a strain in the relationship between Jesus and his family, we might dismiss it as ambiguous at best. However, when Jesus' mother and brothers arrived, they did not receive a warm reception. Rather, upon reaching the house where Jesus was staying, they stood outside and sent in to him to call him out (Mark 3:31). That they did not or could not enter a house in which their son was staying seems odd to us, but it makes sense if the home where Jesus was staying was an Essene-like house into which outsiders could not go. If this was the case, the fact that they didn't go inside does not necessarily indicate a strained relationship. However, it is Jesus' next words which tell the story, for when Jesus was told that his family was outside, he ignored them and said:

> "Who are my mother and my brothers?" And looking at those who sat around him he said, "Here are my mother and my brothers! Whoever does the will of God is my brother and my sister and my mother!"
> — Mark 3:34-35

This does not seem like something we would expect someone — especially Jesus — to say, at least without some follow-up or resolution such as then going out to kiss his mother and speak with the family, but Mark didn't report that Jesus greeted or spoke to them at all. Instead, the episode abruptly ends without resolution — as if Jesus is giving a silent slap to his family's face, indicating that there was some distance or even animosity between Jesus and his family. Another slap is seen in the fact that Mark did not mention any family member by name — not even Jesus' mother.

The context of this story may also give a clue as to Mark's intent, as Mark placed the parable of the sower immediately following this episode. In that parable, seed was scattered on various kinds of soil. Most of the seed falls on soil which does not allow it to take root and grow. Jesus goes on to explain that the seed is "the word" which many will not understand and accept. "Let those who have ears, hear."

Mark may have placed this parable here for a reason. Coming as it does after Jesus "snubs" his family, could it be Mark's way of saying that he considered Jesus' family to be among those who "would not receive the word"? Let those who have ears to hear, hear.

Rejected at Nazareth

The only other time Mark mentioned Jesus' family was when Jesus visited his hometown. This time it was Jesus who is not received warmly:

> He left that place and came to his hometown, and his disciples followed him. On the sabbath he began to teach in the synagogue, and many who heard him were astounded. They said, "Where did this man get all this? What is this wisdom that has been given to him? What deeds of power are being done by his hands! Is not this the carpenter, the son of Mary and brother of James and Joses and Judas and Simon, and are not his sisters here with us?" And they took offense at him. Then Jesus said to them, "Prophets are not without honor, except in their hometown, and among their own kin, and in their own house." And he could do no deed of power there, except that he laid his hands on a few sick people and cured them. And he was amazed at their unbelief.
> — Mark 6:1-6a

This episode comes just after Mark had reported three miracles in which people who were unclean had been healed by Jesus — the man filled with demons who lived among the graves (touching the dead would make someone ritually unclean), a woman who had been menstruating constantly for twelve years (a woman in her menstrual cycle was also ritually unclean), and a girl who been pronounced dead (again, touching the dead would make someone unclean). Those who had witnessed, or had been the subject of, these miracles were reportedly amazed (Mark 5:20 and 5:42).

In the light of these miracles, when Jesus arrived in his hometown (Mark does not name Jesus' hometown here, but he calls Jesus "of Nazareth" several times throughout the gospel), we would expect him to receive, if not a hero's welcome, at least a warm reception, and at first he seemed to get one. In fact, those who heard him were *ekseplessonto*, which the NRSV translates as "astounded," but which can also be rendered as "amazed" or "overwhelmed," and they said words that appear to be of praise and admiration: *"Where did this man get all this? What is this wisdom that has been given to him? What deeds of power are being done by his hands!"* However, Mark then reported that they "took offense" at him. (The word translated as "they took offense" is the Greek word *eskandalizonto*, which could also be translated as "they were scandalized" by him.)

Once this "offensive" reaction was expressed, the preceding words of seeming praise take on a sarcastic twist. Apparently the townsfolk were unimpressed by Jesus and his ministry.

What was it that caused them to reject Jesus? Was it something that Jesus said? After all, Jesus had just taught in the synagogue. Mark, however, did not report the content of Jesus' teaching that day, so that does not seem to be the reason.

More likely, it had something to do with Jesus' family, for both the family and the offense were mentioned in the same verse. This was the only time Mark referred to any of Jesus' family by name:

> Is this not the carpenter, the son of Mary and the brother of James and Joses and Judas and Simon? And are not his sisters here with us? And they took offense at him.
> — Mark 6:3

One explanation may be that the townspeople considered it offensive that Jesus — a mere carpenter — presumed to teach them. Mark, by the way, was the only gospel writer to call Jesus a carpenter — a profession he could continue to practice if he was, or had been, an Essene. Matthew amended this passage to read "Is this not the carpenter's son...?" and thus became the only gospel to mention that Joseph was a carpenter. It is interesting to note that Mark never mentioned a father of Jesus (more on this below).

It may be possible that Jesus' family was not held in high esteem by their neighbors, and by extension Jesus' hometown folk were therefore unimpressed or even offended by Jesus.

However, we also may be misreading exactly who is offended here.

One of the problems in interpreting a scripture passage is that biblical Greek does not have quotation marks. It is often clear where a speech began by the use of the words "he said," but it is less clear where a speech ended. In this passage, the speech by Jesus' critics began halfway through verse 2, after the words "they said." It is also clear where Jesus' response began, in verse 4.

But where does the speech beginning in verse 2 end? Translators normally put the quotation marks after the reference to the sisters before the end of verse 3. However, in light of the family's attitude toward Jesus in the episode in which Jesus was deemed to be out of his mind, it may be that the quotation continues through the end of the verse. This would mean that the "they" of this verse was not the townspeople but the family of Jesus. If this is the case, it is Jesus' own family who took offense at, or perhaps more appropriately, were scandalized by, Jesus. If so, the townspeople would have been using Jesus' own family as witnesses against him! Furthermore, Mark made a point of saying that Jesus' family was "with" the townsfolk, not "with" Jesus — and if Jesus' own family didn't think highly of him, their attitude may have influenced the attitude of the townsfolk, as well.

Wherever one may choose to put the quotation marks, however, it seems that Luke apparently thought it was Mark's intent to portray Jesus' family as critical of

Jesus here, for when Luke reported the visit of Jesus to Nazareth he left out words that could be construed as negative toward Jesus' family. In fact, he didn't mention the family of Jesus in this episode at all.

Without Honor in His Own Family and House
Consider also Jesus' response to the rejection in Nazareth:

> Then Jesus said to them "Prophets are not without honor, except in their hometown, and among their own kin, and in their own house."
> — Mark 6:4

Do not be deceived about the nuance of the translation of the NRSV. By saying that a prophet is not without honor "in" his hometown and "among" his kin, we might get the sense that two different words are used in the Greek and that Mark was saying something different about the way Jesus' family felt about him as opposed to his neighbors. However, this is not the case, and an examination of the original Greek is helpful here. The word which the NRSV translators render in this proverb as "in" and "among" is the Greek preposition *ev*. It is the most common preposition in the New Testament and can be used with a variety of meanings, depending on the context. Most often it means "in" but it can also be translated as "among" or "with" or "by," among others, so any of those renderings are "correct." However, the context here is a proverb in which the same word is used the same way three times in a row:

> *en* his own hometown,
> and *en* his own family,
> and *en* his own house.

However the word is rendered, Mark's intent seems to indicate that it was not just Jesus' neighbors but also Jesus' own family who were among those who did not hold Jesus in high esteem. Luke certainly believed this to be Mark's intent, for when Luke recorded this same proverb he left out the reference to Jesus' kin and house: "Truly I tell you, no prophet is accepted in the prophet's own hometown" (Luke 4:24).

The Family's Unbelief
Mark then wrote these words:

> And he could do no deed of power there, except that he laid his hands on a few sick people and cured them. And he was amazed at their unbelief.
> — Mark 6:5-6

Again, the "they" at whom Jesus was amazed because of their unbelief may actually have included Jesus' own family! It is important to note that Mark was not the only gospel writer to admit to the unbelief of Jesus' family, as John also reported that Jesus' own brothers did not believe in him during his lifetime.

Jesus' Rejection — Not *at* Nazareth but *of* Nazareth and His Family
Finally, just as Mark placed the parable of the sower after the first encounter with Jesus' family as a way of critiquing them, he put a story immediately after the rejection at Nazareth which does the same thing. In this story Mark reported that Jesus sent his disciples out two by two, saying to them:

> Wherever you enter a house, stay there until you leave the place. If any place will not welcome you and they refuse to

hear you, as you leave, shake off the dust that is on your feet
as a testimony against them.
— Mark 6:10-11

By reporting this mission of the disciples immediately
after the hometown rejection, Mark may have been de-
picting Jesus as shaking the dust of Nazareth — and his
family — from his own feet — and Mark never mentioned
Jesus' family again.

Mary
Many readers of the Bible find it odd that Mark nowhere
depicted Mary in a favorable light. Matthew and Luke,
of course, included her in the infancy narratives, and she
played a particularly important and positive role in Luke's
account of the birth of Jesus. John's gospel has no infancy
narrative, but John included Mary several times throughout his narrative in ways the others did not, even placing
her in Jerusalem at the feet of Jesus when he was crucified. Luke didn't place her at the crucifixion, but in Acts
he did report that she was in Jerusalem, along with Jesus'
brothers, immediately after the resurrection and before
Pentecost.

Mark, however, included no birth stories — perhaps
because of an Ebionite-like belief in the "adoption" rather
than the divine birth of Jesus. Neither did he place Mary
in the passion narrative, nor at the cross. Interestingly,
when Mark reported that there were women who "from a
distance" witnessed the crucifixion (Mark 15:40), he mentioned three of them by name. Two were named Mary
— but Jesus' mother was not one of them. The truth is,
Mary appeared but twice in Mark and was mentioned by
name only once in his entire gospel. Compared with the
other gospel writers, she is conspicuously absent.

Joseph?

Speaking of conspicuous absences, I have already noted that a father of Jesus never appears in Mark. He was not with Jesus' "mother and brothers" when they came for him in Capernaum, nor was he present in Nazareth when Jesus returned to his hometown. Mark never even mentioned a father, let alone gave him a name. If Mark was our only witness, we would know nothing of Jesus' father.

The absence of a father in Mark is sometimes explained with the suggestion that he may have already died by the time Jesus reached adulthood. However, John — who, like Mark, has no infancy narrative — not only identified the father of Jesus as Joseph, he also spoke of him in a way that indicated that he was still alive when Jesus was an adult. ("Is this not Jesus, the son of Joseph, whose father and mother we know?" [John 6:42]) Why Mark failed to mention him remains a mystery.

Mark, however, did mention *another* Joseph — Joseph of Arimathea (the only Joseph mentioned in Mark — although Mark did say that Jesus had a brother named Joses, which is a Greek variant of Joseph).

A few notes about Joseph of Arimathea:

• There is no record of a town called "Arimathea." It has been suggested that the name Arimathea was a Greek transliteration of the Hebrew word for the city Ramathaim-Zophim, also called Ramah that had been the birthplace and home of the prophet Samuel, not too far from Jerusalem (Luke called Arimathea a town of Judea).
• The only time that he is mentioned in the gospel of Mark was when he claimed the body of Jesus.
• Whereas the NRSV translation states that Joseph was "a respected member of the council," a literal translation of the Greek would render those words "a counselor of

high standing" or "prominence." Mark did not call him rich, although if he was a successful counselor we might expect him to have had a high income. However, if he was a member of an order such as the Essenes which pooled its income, he would not be "wealthy" in the traditional sense — and the word "high standing" has implications that reach beyond wealth.

- Although Luke called Joseph a member of the council which interrogated Jesus, Mark did not. When Mark referred to Jesus' interrogation, he used the word "Sanhedrin" (Mark 14:55 and 15:1), which was a council made up of 71 people who came from the families of the chief priest, the scribes, and the lay elders — just the group Jesus had said would reject him and hand him over for death. It is possible that Joseph was a member of the Sanhedrin, but Mark did not so indicate, only calling him a "counselor of high standing, who was also himself waiting expectantly for the kingdom of God..." (Mark 15:43).
- When Joseph claimed Jesus' body for burial, Mark told us that he wrapped it in a "linen" cloth — the same cloth worn by Essenes and by the young man in the garden.

In the absence of a father in the gospel of Mark, it is possible that Joseph of Arimathea was something of an "adoptive" father in the order of those "seeking the kingdom of heaven" (the Essenes?), and that he was performing a "fatherly" duty in claiming and burying the body of Jesus.

An Anti-Family Bias?

We rarely point out that Jesus' brothers did not believe in him during his lifetime, nor do we want to consider that Mark intentionally depicted Jesus' parents in a negative light. Influenced as we are by other gospels — especially the infancy narratives — along with the way we depict the Christmas story in our churches (and perhaps also our own desire to see Jesus' family in a positive light), we generally characterize his family — especially his mother and father — as loving and supportive.

However, we are not reading the other gospels, nor are we to try to re-create Jesus in *our* image. We are reading Mark, and we must focus on how *Mark* depicted Jesus' family — and that was decidedly unfavorable.

As to why Mark presented them that way, we shall discover that he had his reasons — but first let's turn to the disciples.

The Disciples
Unlike the family of Jesus, Mark depicted the disciples in a favorable way — at least at first. After all, Mark could not deny the role and importance of the disciples in the ministry of Jesus, and something very positive is seen in their choice to give up everything and follow. Furthermore, they had credibility simply because Jesus himself selected them. As we shall see, however, Mark quickly began to undermine that credibility.

The Twelve
That Jesus chose twelve to be with him is affirmed by all the gospel writers as well as by Paul — although Paul never named them, and he specifically mentioned "the twelve" only once, when he was cataloguing the list of those who had seen the risen Lord (1 Corinthians 15:5). John also never gave a list of their names, although he did mention at least seven of the twelve by name at various points of his gospel.

Jesus didn't start with twelve, however. He started with four, all fishermen: Peter and his brother Andrew, plus James and John the sons of Zebedee. The initial role of those two sets of brothers is mentioned by Mark in the very first chapter, when Jesus said to Peter and Andrew: "Follow me and I will make you fish for people" (Mark 1:17).

Initial Role: Apprentices

What that phrase means is revealed later in chapter 1. Jesus had already performed his first miracle as reported by Mark — the exorcism of a man with an "unclean spirit" in a synagogue on the sabbath. Upon leaving the synagogue, "They entered the home of Simon and Andrew, with James and John." Simon's mother-in-law was in bed with a fever. Jesus healed her of the fever, and Mark told us "she began to serve them" (Mark 1:31).

Mark then wrote: "That evening at sunset, they brought to him all who were sick or possessed with demons" (Mark 1:32). Although Mark didn't specifically say who the "they" were, we can be sure that Peter, Andrew, James, and John — the four newly called disciples — were among them. Instead of casting nets out into the water to bring fish into their boats, they were casting about the city to bring people to Jesus to be healed.

The word "disciple" is the Greek word *mathete*. This word can be variously translated as "learner," "pupil," "apprentice," "disciple," or "adherent," depending on the context. If Jesus was using anything like an Essene model of taking on the children of other people as students (even if he himself was not an Essene), we might consider the disciples at this point to be pupils of or apprentices to Jesus as much as anything else. Among other things, their role at this point was one of front men for Jesus: Jesus would go into a town, and the *mathete* would bring to him people who needed to be healed.

From Apprentices to Apostles

Mark reported that people were soon coming to Jesus not only from Galilee, but also "in great numbers from Judea, Jerusalem, Idumea (south of Judea), beyond the Jordan (Perea), and the region around Tyre and Sidon" (Mark 3:8). As the crowds grew, so apparently did the need for those who would do what Jesus himself was doing. Therefore, from those who were following him, Jesus selected "twelve, whom he also named apostles, to be with him and to be sent out to proclaim the message, and to have authority to cast out demons" (Mark 3:14-15) — precisely what Jesus himself had been doing up to that point.

The word "apostle" means "one who is sent." Interestingly, Mark only reported one time when Jesus sent them out in this way (Mark 6:7). It is also the only other time he used the word "apostle" in relation to the twelve.

Jesus' New "Family"

"The twelve" was used in relation to this group nine other times in Mark (four of them during Holy Week). The word "disciples" was also used, sometimes referring not only to the twelve but also to others who followed Jesus. In any event, the disciples (whether "the twelve" and/or others) became what we might call Jesus' "new family."

This is made clear in the passage immediately following the naming of the twelve, a passage we have already mentioned in another context:

> Looking at those who sat around him, he said, "Here are my mother and my brothers! Whoever does the will of God is my brother and sister and mother."
> — Mark 3:34-35

It seems apparent that Jesus and his disciples were following an Essene-like model of leaving the biological family and becoming part of a new community, in which the members pool their property and income. Whether or not Jesus was an Essene himself is not the point — it is this model of community in which he participated.

Although Mark reported that Jesus only selected males as members of "the twelve," it is clear that Jesus also included women in his "family." For one thing, he specifically mentioned women in his response about family: "Whoever does the will of God is my brother and my *sister* and my *mother*" (Mark 3:35, emphasis mine). Second, when Mark mentioned those who witnessed the crucifixion, he mentioned "women looking on from a distance; among them were Mary Magdalene and Mary the mother of James the younger and of Joses, and Salome. They used to follow him and provided for him when he was in Galilee; and there were many other women who had come up with him to Jerusalem" (Mark 15:40-41).

The Inner Circle
Of the twelve, only the names of Peter, Andrew, James, and John are mentioned more than once in Mark's gospel narrative (except for Judas Iscariot, who was mentioned again in the passion narrative). These sets of brothers (and sometimes only Peter, James, and John) came to form an "inner circle" within the twelve. It was only Peter, James, and John, for example, who went with Jesus "up a high mountain" to witness his "transfiguration"; it was only Peter, James, John, and Andrew to whom Jesus spoke the words of the "little apocalypse"; and it was only James, John, and Peter whom Jesus took apart from the others and told them to watch while he prayed in the Garden of Gethsemane.

Theme of Misunderstanding

However, Mark began to undermine the credibility of the disciples, including the inner circle, and revealed a distance between Jesus and his disciples not unlike what we saw between Jesus and his family. The first hint was in the explanation of the parable of the sower. Although the parable is relatively simple and easy to understand, Jesus had to spell it out for them. "Do you not understand this parable?" he asked, incredulously. "Then how will you understand all the parables?" (Mark 4:13).

This theme of misunderstanding pervaded the gospel:

- After the walking on the water, Mark wrote: "And they (the disciples) did not understand about the loaves, but their hearts were hardened" (Mark 6:52);
- When the disciples asked about the teaching regarding what defiled, Jesus asked: "Then do you also fail to understand?" (Mark 7:18);
- After the feeding of the 4,000, Jesus again asked: "Do you still not perceive or understand? Are your hearts hardened? Do you have eyes and fail to see? Do you have ears, and fail to hear? And do you not remember? ... Do you not yet understand?" (Mark 8:17-21);
- After the second passion prediction the disciples not only didn't understand, but Mark described their relationship with Jesus in a way we would not expect with people who were supposedly close: "They did not understand what he was saying and were *afraid* to ask him" (Mark 8:32; emphasis mine).

Peter

Nowhere, however, is the undermining of the credibility of the disciples seen more forcefully than in the person of Peter. This is seen especially in the episode in which

Peter became the first person to recognize Jesus as the messiah (Mark 8:39), which we generally see as a "good confession." However, Mark's account of this confession stands in stark contrast to Matthew's and Luke's versions of this same incident.

As opposed to Matthew, for example, Mark did not report that Peter called Jesus "the Son of the living God" (nor does Mark report that any human being called Jesus "Son of God," for that matter, until the centurion standing at the foot of the cross did so upon Jesus' death). Furthermore, Mark did not report that Jesus lauded Peter for his insight ("Blessed are you, Simon son of Jonah!" Matthew 16:17), nor did he say that Jesus gave Peter authority (the keys to the kingdom) over the church (a word Mark never used). Whereas Matthew reported that Jesus gave Simon the surname Peter because of his insight, Mark did not (although Mark had reported earlier, at the naming of the twelve, that Jesus surnamed Simon with the name Peter, but without giving a reason).

Of course, Mark did report a new name that Jesus gave Peter in this passage, but it wasn't "Rock." It came after Jesus, for the first time, explained that he would "undergo great suffering, and be rejected by the elders, the chief priests and the scribes, and be killed, and after three days rise again" (Mark 8:31). Upon hearing this, Peter rebuked Jesus (Mark 8:32). Jesus in turn rebuked Peter, saying: "Get behind me, Satan!" (Mark 8:33).

Mark reiterated this rebuke and intensified it by immediately reporting that Jesus called together a crowd and uttered these words:

> Those who are ashamed of me and of my words in this adulterous and sinful generation, of them the Son of Man will also be ashamed when he comes in the glory of his Father with the holy angels.
> — Mark 8:38

It is interesting to note that Luke omitted the passage in which Jesus rebuked and called Peter "Satan." In fact, every step of the way, where Mark discredited Peter, Luke rehabilitated him (similar to the way Luke changed Mark's discrediting of the family):

- Here, where Luke omitted Peter's rebuke of Jesus, Luke also omitted Jesus' rebuke of Peter, and did not have Jesus call Peter "Satan";
- At the Last Supper, when Jesus said that Peter would deny him three times, Luke added that Jesus also foretold that Peter would "turn back," and when he did, he was to "strengthen" his brothers — a statement Mark lacked; and
- Whereas Mark had no post-resurrection appearances, Luke affirmed that Jesus appeared to Simon on the first day after the sabbath.

An Anti-Family, Anti-Disciple Bias?

From what has been observed as to how Mark portrayed both the family of Jesus and the disciples, a case can be made that Mark had an underlying anti-family and anti-disciple bias of Jesus.

Why would Mark display such an animus against the family of Jesus or the disciples?

Could the answer lie in the fact that both of these groups — the disciples and the family of Jesus — had leadership roles in the early church: the disciples — and especially Peter — as the founders of the church; and Jesus' family — and especially James — in leading the church in Jerusalem? Could it be that Mark belonged to a group that opposed the leadership of these groups, even as he maintained allegiance to Jesus?

And did political divisions and differences within the early church play a part in Mark's anti-family, anti-disciple bias? Did they have anything to do with Mark's decision to omit resurrection appearances after the story of the empty tomb?

What was going on in the leadership of the church at the time during which Mark wrote?

Leadership in the Early Church

Whereas Mark told the disciples to go to Galilee, Luke centered the story of the early church in Jerusalem. After the resurrection, according to Luke, the disciples did not go to Galilee. Instead, they stayed in Jerusalem, where the church began on Pentecost and where the first Essene-like community was located ("All who believed were together and had all things in common; they would sell their possessions and goods and distribute the proceeds to all, as any had need." [Acts 2:44-45]). At this point, Peter was clearly the leader. Because he traveled, however (as apparently did the other apostles — at least those who were not immediately martyred), a leadership void was left in Jerusalem. This void was filled by James, the brother of the Lord.

James' leadership role was seen most tellingly in the debate about whether Gentiles should have to undergo circumcision or not. Luke told us that all the apostles and elders, including Peter and Paul, met to consider the matter. After all sides are heard, however, it was James who rendered the verdict, saying: "Therefore I have reached the decision..." (Acts 15:19).

Luke reaffirmed the leadership of James again when Paul returned to Jerusalem before his arrest and trip to Rome. Luke wrote that when Paul arrived he met with all the elders, but only James was mentioned by name — presumably because of the position of authority that he held within the church.

Luke was not the only biblical witness to James' leadership role in the Jerusalem church. Paul corroborated this, as well, in Galatians 1:18, when he recalled his first visit to Jerusalem three years after his call to preach among the Gentiles. In that visit, he said, he stayed with Peter for fifteen days, and "did not see any other apostle except James the Lord's brother." It is important to note that Paul deemed James an apostle, calling him one of the "acknowledged pillars" (Galatians 2:9) even though James was not one of the disciples, nor did James play any significant role during the earthly life of Jesus.

Why James?

That Peter was a leader in the church seems appropriate. After all, he was one of the twelve and a member of Jesus' "inner circle." But why James? He was barely mentioned in the gospel story at all, and when he was, it was not in the most favorable light. John's gospel even stated that Jesus' brothers — presumably including James — did not believe in Jesus during his earthly ministry (John 7:5).

James' pathway to apostleship, however, was revealed to us by Paul, in his account of those to whom Jesus had appeared:

> For I handed on to you as of first importance what I in turn had received: that Christ died for our sins in accordance with the scriptures, and that he was buried, and that he was raised on the third day in accordance with the scriptures, and that he appeared to Cephas, then to the twelve. Then he appeared to more than five hundred brothers and sisters at one time, most of whom are still alive, though some have died. Then he appeared to **James** (emphasis mine), then to all the apostles.
> — 1 Corinthians 15:3-7

James' authority evidently came from the fact that Jesus appeared to him after the resurrection. Because of this he not only became a steadfast believer and supporter of the ministry but it gave him the credentials he needed for leadership in the Jerusalem church.

Mark, of course, did not report any post-resurrection appearances, let alone one to James. Was Mark unaware of this tradition — or did he omit it for a reason?

The Death of James and the Crisis of Succession

There is no mention of the death of James in the Bible. He was apparently still alive when Luke reported that Paul departed for Rome in about AD 60 — the year Festus was appointed procurator of Judea. Once Paul left for Rome, Luke made no mention of James, or any events in Jerusalem, after that. The Bible is silent on the fate of James.

We gain some information, however, from one Hegesippus (c. AD 110–c. AD 180), a bishop who was a chronicler of church history, who wrote that James was martyred by stoning in Jerusalem before the fall of Jerusalem. Josephus also mentioned this in his *Jewish Antiquities*, stating that James died by stoning at the hands of the high priest Ananus. Some have questioned the authenticity of this citation, thinking it too insignificant an event to have been noticed by Josephus, and that it must have been inserted by later Christian copyists. However, it has been found in every ancient copy of Josephus' book — including translations in other languages — so many consider it to be authentic.

Whether Josephus' reference is authentic or not, however, James had to die sometime, and his death would likely have triggered a "crisis of succession" in the early church. This, in fact, is what occurred, according to church historian Eusebius of Caesarea, writing around AD 300 (and who used Hegesippus as a source):

After the martyrdom of James and the conquest of Jerusalem which immediately followed, it is said that those of the apostles and disciples of the Lord that were still living came together from all directions with those that were related to the Lord according to the flesh (for the majority of them also were still alive) to take counsel as to who was worthy to succeed James. They all with one consent pronounced Symeon, the son of Clopas, of whom the gospel also makes mention; to be worthy of the episcopal throne of that parish. He was a cousin, as they say, of the Saviour. For Hegesippus records that Clopas was a brother of Joseph.
(Eusebius, *Church History*, Book III, Chapter 11)

But not everyone was happy.

According to Hegesippus, a man named Thebutis (or Thebulis) felt that he should have been elected, and when he wasn't, he began to foment dissension within the church. We know nothing of Thebutis other than this.

It is important to note the groups that made the decision as to who would become the new leader in Jerusalem: 1) the disciples of the Lord, and 2) the blood relatives of the Lord (the family of Jesus). Not only that, if Simeon was a cousin to Jesus, the leadership role was "staying within the family."

If Mark was a supporter of someone other than Simeon to lead the church, it cannot be coincidence that these are precisely the groups that Mark portrayed in an unfavorable light in his gospel (and if Joseph was a blood relative of Simeon, this may be a reason Mark omitted him from the narrative, as well). This indicates a division between Mark and those groups.

That there were such divisions within the early church, even well before Mark wrote, is not in question. Luke, for example, referred to the controversy within the early church over the practice of circumcision: "Certain individuals came down from Judea and were teaching the brothers, 'Unless you are circumcised according to the custom of Moses, you cannot be saved' " (Acts 15:1ff).

We have already noted that Paul — writing before both Mark and Luke — referred to these divisions, as well — most famously in his first letter to Corinth:

> For it has been reported to me by Chloe's people that there are quarrels among you, my brothers and sisters. What I mean is that each of you says, "I belong to Paul," or "I belong to Apollos," or "I belong to Cephas," or "I belong to Christ." Has Christ been divided?
> — 1 Corinthians 1:10-13a

We can assume that the party of Peter referred to those who aligned themselves with Peter, and more broadly, "the disciples of the Lord." The party of Paul may refer to the Gentile Christians who did not believe in the need for circumcision. The party of Apollos may have referred to those who came to the faith through a man whom Luke called an eloquent Egyptian-born Jew who believed Jesus to be the messiah, but who "knew only the baptism of John" (Acts 18:24ff).

But who was the "party of Christ"? Did not those who followed Paul or Peter or Apollos or others also "belong" to Christ?

At one time I thought that this term applied to those who considered themselves to be the true believers not tied to any one person or group. However, in light of what Hegesippus tells us, the group of blood relatives of Jesus who were part of the leadership group of the church fit perfectly those who might call themselves the "party of Christ."

The Party of Thebutis?

What about Thebutis? Was there a party of Thebutis? After the death of James, were there those who said

"We belong to Thebutis" the way others earlier had said they belonged to Paul, Peter, Apollos, or Christ? Did Mark belong to a group that considered Thebutis to be their leader and who wanted him or someone like him to be the new head of the church in Jerusalem? Did the words "go to Galilee" mean that Mark didn't side with the Jerusalem church but with a group that had left Jerusalem, as Thebutis may have done after his rejection by the church? The timing of Mark's writing of his gospel, along with the way he portrayed the disciples and the family of Jesus, may suggest such a scenario.

The Unknown Exorcist

Furthermore, Mark himself acknowledged such divisions even within the pages of his gospel. Consider the story of the unknown exorcist reported in Mark 9:38:

> John said to him, "Teacher, we saw someone casting out demons in your name, and we tried to stop him, because he was not following us."

It is interesting to note that Mark told us Jesus said that people such as this, who were "not following us" were not only not to be opposed but they should be considered important to the movement:

> But Jesus said, "Do not stop him; for no one who does a deed of power in my name will be able soon afterward to speak evil of me. Whoever is not against us is for us. For truly I tell you, whoever gives you a cup of water to drink because you bear the name of Christ will by no means lose the reward."
> — Mark 9:39-41

Is it possible that Mark had Thebutis in mind when he decided to include this passage? It is impossible to know for sure. We can assume, however, that Mark included this episode for a reason, and we can conjecture that the reason was to address divisions within the church that existed when Mark wrote his gospel. Furthermore, even without affirming that Mark sided with Thebutis (or that he was an Essene or Ebionite or a member of any other specific party), we can at the least affirm that Mark did not belong to the party of the disciples or the blood relatives of Jesus.

No Resurrection Appearances!

What could the omission of resurrection appearances after the story of the empty tomb possibly have to do with a political dispute within the early church? The answer may be "quite a bit," considering that the resurrection appearances of Jesus to the disciples and James is what gave them their authority in the first place.

As we have seen, the first generation of the Jerusalem church was led by the disciples and family of Jesus. If their authority over the church was derived — in part, at least — from the fact that Jesus had appeared to them, perhaps Mark felt that one way to try to discredit and undermine that authority would be not to highlight the very appearances that gave them that authority in the first place.

Lest we think it disingenuous for Mark to eliminate post-resurrection appearances of Jesus from the story for political (or any) reason, especially in the face of such a strong tradition affirming them, we must acknowledge that this would not be the first (or the last) time revisionist history had been written in order to make a point. It wasn't even the first time it had been done in the Bible.

Consider the histories of the reigns of the kings of Israel and Judah that are found in the Old Testament. These histories are told twice: first in the Deuteronomic history found in 1 Samuel through 2 Kings; again by the chronicler in 1 and 2 Chronicles. Both histories recounted stories of the kings that ruled over Judah, and both dealt extensively with the importance of David as the quintessential leader and ideal king of Israel. Each one, however, emphasized different parts of the story and told the story a little differently.

For example, perhaps no episodes in the life of David are more well-known than the stories of David's slaying of Goliath and his sin with Bathsheba. Both of these stories are found in the Deuteronomic history — David and Goliath in 1 Samuel 17, and David and Bathsheba in 2 Samuel 11 and 12. The chronicler, however, omitted both. In fact, the name of Bathsheba, mother of Solomon, never appears in Chronicles, and Goliath's name only figured incidentally when he was mentioned as the brother of a certain Lahmi who was slain by a man named Jair (1 Chronicles 20:5).

Did the chronicler think that by omitting these stories and/or characters that he would somehow be able to erase them from history? Probably not — in fact, we still talk about them even today — but these stories apparently did not contribute to the points he wanted to make about David as he wrote about leadership issues facing the post-exilic Hebrew community, so he didn't include them.

In a similar manner, I am suggesting that the post-resurrection appearances of Jesus did not contribute to the point Mark was trying to make regarding the leadership issues facing the church of his day, so he chose not to include them. Indeed, Matthew and Luke did something of the same thing when they wrote their gospels. Although they had Mark in front of them when they wrote, they changed Mark by addition, subtraction, and/or revision, as we have seen.

But understand this clearly: Mark was not saying that the risen Jesus did not appear. Neither did he deny the reality of the resurrection, nor does it seem he would want to, since he concluded his gospel with the announcement that Jesus was risen and had woven appearances of the risen Lord into the very fabric of his gospel. Mark believed in the resurrection.

I believe that Mark had consciously chosen to not report post-resurrection appearances of Jesus in his gospel, and of all the reasons we have explored in this study, it seems to me the best reason for that omission relates to Mark's politics within the church. If the disciples and the family of Jesus derived their authority from these appearances — not because they believed in Jesus (after all, many people believed in him) but because the risen Lord had appeared to them — by not reporting these appearances Mark might be making a political statement trying to undermine their authority, and especially their authority to select the new head of the church. Furthermore, if Mark, writing shortly after this selection, disagreed with the choices they had made, by omitting post-resurrection appearances to them — combined with his negative portrayal of them in his gospel — he may also have been trying to undermine the legitimacy of their newly appointed successor. Of all the reasons we have explored, I believe this best explains Mark's motives for omitting resurrection appearances after the story of the empty tomb.

One Final Note
Although the other gospel writers and Paul reported post-resurrection appearances of Jesus, the truth is there is no unanimity among them regarding those appearances. Each gospel writer reported different stories, and none of them reported the appearance to the 500 or the appearance to James mentioned by Paul. It would seem that each gospel writer selected and omitted the stories that made the points he (or she) wished to make — and

there were probably many such stories in circulation from which to choose.

Those who remember the time after the death of Elvis Presley may appreciate this. Elvis was an iconic and charismatic figure — much loved and adored by his many fans. When he died, many saw it as a personal loss — like losing a family member. As one of the stages of grief is denial, it was natural, I suppose, for those who loved and adored Elvis to experience that stage of grief just like anyone else. Many people simply refused to believe that Elvis Presley was dead.

But who would have believed the stories that followed! How many "Elvis sightings" were there? How many articles were there in newspapers and magazines of people who had claimed to have seen Elvis after his death? Several books were written on the subject, many of them not trying to debunk the sightings but rather to authenticate them. Several television specials around the subject were produced, including *The Elvis Files* in 1991, and *The Elvis Conspiracy* in 1992 — fifteen years after Elvis' death. Even today, almost forty years after his death, there are people who still believe that Elvis did not die in 1977, but just went into hiding.

Most people today, of course, do believe that Elvis died in 1977, and that the so-called sightings of Elvis are just that — so-called — and were either made by people who were mistaken or who were seeking publicity.

Now think of the trouble Mark and the other gospel writers may have had (in an age without TV, video, DNA testing, and the like) in discerning which appearance stories of Jesus were true and which were false — forty years and more after Jesus' death — and which ones to use (or not to use) to make the points they wanted to make about Jesus, and to make sense of the situation of the early church.

Maybe Mark chose not to report any, for fear of including some that may not have been true!

Why do *you* think he didn't report them?

Conclusion

Why Mark?

If Mark, among other things, was anti-family, anti-disciples, anti-virgin birth, and didn't have appearances of Jesus after the resurrection, why did subsequent generations include his gospel in the canon in the first place?

Part of the answer, I believe, has to do with the way Mark crafted his gospel — artisan that he was. His treatment of Jesus' family and of the disciples, though not flattering, was subtle, and although he did not include stories of the virgin birth, he didn't explicitly deny these stories, either. Furthermore, he had the imprimatur of Papias and others who considered him to have been a companion to Peter. Most importantly, Matthew and Luke had "endorsed" Mark by using his gospel as a template for their own.

However, if Mark's gospel in any way represented a significant splinter or fringe group within the early church, it may have been included in the canon for another reason: in order to help keep this group within the fellowship. After all, what better way to draw them into the circle than to co-opt their "book" and include it as a part of the larger corpus — much the same way major political parties today might include planks of minority parties in their platforms in order to attract members of those groups to join them.

The "best" answer, I suppose, may be that the early church knew that Mark — despite any political differences he may have had with others — loved and respected Jesus — Son of God and Son of Man, preacher of the good news of the kingdom of God, one who cast out demons,

Messiah, suffering servant, and risen Lord. When they read Mark's gospel and saw the way Jesus cared for outcasts and sinners, the unclean, and the sick and disabled, they saw something of themselves. So do we. When they read of the foibles and even failures of the family of Jesus and his disciples, they saw a bit of themselves. So do we. And when they "went to Galilee" and read the gospel story, empowered by the Holy Spirit, they encountered the risen Lord — and so do we!